JESUS, THE LIVING BREAD

JESUS, THE LIVING BREAD

A Chronicle of the Forty-First International Eucharistic Congress
Philadelphia, Pennsylvania, August 1976

James M. Talley, Supervising Editor

Logos International, Plainfield, New Jersey 07061 U.S.A.

Nihil obstat

    James McGrath, *Censor Librorum*

Imprimatur

    John Cardinal Krol, *Archbishop of Philadelphia*

September 8, 1976

JESUS, THE LIVING BREAD
Copyright © 1976 Logos International
Printed in the United States of America
All rights reserved
International Standard Book Number: 0-88270-199-1
Library of Congress Catalog Card Number: 76-45526
Published by Logos International, Plainfield, New Jersey 07061

To every pilgrim who seeks Jesus

A team of journalists representing the *National Courier*, a Christian newspaper published by Logos International Fellowship, Inc., gathered the information and the photographs for this spiritual anthology of a very special occasion in Philadelphia, Pennsylvania, U.S.A.

Editor-Coordinator/James M. Talley
Senior Contributing Writer/William Proctor
Director of Design-Photography/John Murello
Senior Staff Writer/Dorianne Perrucci
Contributing Writer/Robert Armbruster
Photographer/Richard Taylor
Photographer/Craig Callan
Photographer/Thurman Mason
Photographer/Stephen J. Allen
Photographer's Assistant/Jane Taylor
Picture Editors/Murello, Perrucci
Consultant/Joseph Orsini
Production Manager/Salvatore Buonocore

The team wishes to acknowledge with gratitude special assistance from the Rev. Msgr. Walter J. Conway, executive secretary of the Congress; Robert H. Palestini, associate executive secretary; Ronald Burns of Gray & Rogers Advertising, Inc.; and Sister Mary Maurice Boyle, who was Sacristan at the Civic Center. A special page at the end of the book lists all the persons who were responsible for the management and execution of a magnificent Congress.

CONTENTS

'Where two or three are gathered in my name...'

For nearly a year, the news spread around the world. In the cities and towns of almost every country on earth both clergy and laity began to think and pray about the event upcoming in America, its theme and the needs it would seek to meet. Through it all, the Lord was at work, ordaining who would attend in person and who would remain behind to pray—a no less important task. As the time drew near, airlines from Europe, Asia, Africa, Australia, and the Americas took on as passengers thousands of the faithful, all of whom were drawn to one city at the calling of their Lord.

A common thirst drew us all—rich and poor, young and old, foreign and native-born Roman Catholics of every color and nationality—and made each of us equal sharers. There was excitement and anticipation as modern day pilgrims came for a celebration. Priests munched sandwiches on the lawn with friends and parishioners. Nuns queued up for Chinese egg rolls and water ices to cool off in the hot Pennsylvania sun. Occasionally, a cardinal or a bishop would wave spontaneously during the solemn

Eucharistic Congress 1926

order of a liturgical procession, or even sit alongside the water fountain outside the Civic Center and talk with other pilgrims.

For eight days in August, Philadelphia truly became "The City of Brotherly Love" it has long been called. Regardless of who we were or where we came from, we received the same invitation to the 41st International Eucharistic Congress: To come and share Jesus, the Living Bread.

Though the Congress was filled with breathtaking beauty and solemn liturgical celebration, it was the song of the new Pentecost—a song first sung at the Second Vatican Council fifteen years ago—

that lifted its simple melody of harmonious love above all the rest.

We again heard the Epistle of Christian Unity first heard at Ephesus 2,000 years ago. And we wept afresh at the command to bring all our brothers and sisters in Christ together in one Body.

It was thus, with both repentance and great joy, that we sat down to talk about our many hungers as a diverse family, and to hear how Jesus, the Living Bread satisfies our hungry hearts.

We can never plan or predict the exact way that God will act in our lives. When Christians meet together for prayer, worship, spiritual learning, and celebration, they may have some idea of the direction that the Holy Spirit will lead them. But, at the same time, they must be prepared for divine surprise, for unexpected, distinctive revelations that will help them further the work of his kingdom.

So it has been with the forty-one International Eucharistic Congresses that have been conducted at far-flung locations around the globe since 1881. Some

years earlier in the mid-nineteenth century, Marie Martha Tamisier, a Frenchwoman from Tours, conceived the idea of the first congress. She reportedly saw two hundred members of the French Parliament dedicate themselves to the Sacred Heart of Jesus during a Eucharistic celebration, and decided such an event would be inspiring to the broader Christian community. So she approached the Bishop of Lille, Monsignor Louis Gaston de Segur, who promptly endorsed the idea and organized a series of Eucharistic

pilgrimages to shrines where Eucharistic miracles had occurred.

It's doubtful that either Mlle. Tamisier or the Bishop of Lille foresaw that God would use these meetings to generate a revival spirit among Catholics which would finally lead to the First International Eucharistic Congress in 1881. But that's exactly what happened. The stated purpose of that first congress, which attracted about 800 pilgrims, was to protest the "torrent of hatred and persecution against Catholicism" and also to "[implant] more firmly than ever Jesus Christ in the souls from which they seek to banish Him," according to a letter circulated by the bishop. He concluded that the "best means of attaining this end is to spread as extensively as possible all Eucharistic works which are best adapted to lead mankind to recover true life and satisfy, at the same time, the justice of God."

Pope Leo XIII heartily approved the idea and thus launched the series of international meetings that have focused on how the real presence of Christ in the bread and wine of Holy Communion can exercise a special spiritual influence in the daily lives of individual Christians. Each congress seems to have communicated its own unique message to the spiritual seekers who congregated from

all parts of the earth. Contemporary Catholics still talk about Pope Paul VI's journey to the 1964 congress in Bombay, for instance, where he visited the poor in Indian slums and talked with Hindu philosophers and leading Indian politicians. It was the first visit by a Roman Pontiff to Asia and the popular press immediately began referring to him as "the missionary pope." A major theme of the Bombay congress—a theme and a congress which Mlle. Tamisier and the Bishop of Lille could probably never have predicted—was the loving outreach of the Church to the Far East and Third World nations. That theme was expanded upon in Bogota and later congresses.

But as the pilgrims streamed into Philadelphia in 1976 for the 41st International Eucharistic Congress, a somewhat different spiritual emphasis seemed to be in the air. Many of the former threads of social concern were still woven into the spiritual fabric of this massive Christian gathering, the first in the United States in fifty years. There were many unresolved problems about the relation of the Church to the poorer peoples of the world; there were many questions about the role of women, and the various minority groups. But underlying all these issues there seemed to be a return to the quest for individual spiritual renewal; a need to reaffirm basic moral values; a fresh drive to establish a firm, personal relationship with Jesus Christ.

Some of the most eager pilgrims in 1976 were the few who had attended the only other International Eucharistic

Eucharistic Congress 1926

Congress in the United States, which was held in Chicago in 1926. They brought to the Philadelphia celebration a sense of perspective that only age and experience can bestow. One of these congress jubilarians was Maryknoll Sister Corde Lorang, who had just taken her vows when she traveled to Chicago in 1926. "I remember the last day when we were all caught in a heavy downpour of rain and hail," she said. "We all got soaked. We wore gray gingham habits in those days."

But the bad weather in Chicago didn't dampen her enthusiasm either for the religious life or for her many secular activities. In the five decades between the two United States congresses, she has contributed to the Maryknoll Inter-

national Cookbook, written two other books, and reported the weather for radio from Ossining, New York.

Sister Corde's main reason for wanting to go to the congress in Philadelphia was "my great devotion to the Blessed Sacrament. It gets to be the absolute center of your life. When you are a religious, you are a bride of Christ, and Christ is there in the Blessed Sacrament. My loyalty is to Him, and his to me. It's a deep union there. I came [to the convent] to help out in his work. The work may be trying, but I never wanted anything else from the time I was in the sixth grade. My personal idea of being a bride of Christ is virginity dedicated to Him. Some people don't agree with that today, but to me, it's a reality. I trust Him. I know He's close."

Possibly because she walks with a cane these days, the 72-year-old Sister Corde was concerned about how she would travel to Philadelphia. At the Chicago congress fifty years before, her father surprised her by financing a trip. In 1976, though, her Heavenly Father was the key. "I kept praying, 'Dear Lord, if you want me there, get me there.' " Another nun soon notified her that her prayers had been answered, and transportation had become available.

The same downpour that drenched Sister Corde in Chicago also caught Father Charles O'Donnell as he was marching in one of the 1926 congress parades. "I was carrying a banner in this big procession when a thunderstorm came along and soaked us," the 80-year-old priest chuckled as he leaned against a post near Independence Hall and watched a similar parade in Philadelphia. "The water got inside the lining of my banner and the whole thing filled up like a hot water bottle. I'll never forget that day."

He said that he had made the journey from his parish in St. Louis to Chicago by an old steam-driven train, and the trip had taken much longer than the flight he had just made from St. Louis to Philadelphia. "You didn't see all these miniskirts in those days," he said with a wink. "The new styles add to the interest. But it was much safer in the cities then than it is now. Most people I knew never locked

Eucharistic Congress 1926

their doors. But in St. Louis where I live now, no priest will even go outside at night, there's so much crime."

Holding a new breviary he had just bought, he said, "This is my last jubilee, my last congress, I know that. At Chicago, I was with a friend of mine who had been a childhood pal, but he's been dead ten years now." Looking wistfully at some of the young men marching by with their huge "Jesus, Bread of Life" banners, Father O'Donnell murmured, "I

could have carried four or five banners in Chicago, but I can't do that now. I was determined I'd get to this congress, though, and it really gives me a great sense of satisfaction. I just thank God I've had the opportunity to attend two of them. Some of the retired priests I live with back in St. Louis have arthritis and other ailments, and they weren't able to make the trip. I'm just thankful I'm here."

Then he shook off his solemn expression and flashed his quick Irish smile: "But this congress shows me the Church is still strong. The fact that they can have something like this, with all these people, lets you know the Church hasn't weakened any. They've taken advantage of modern techniques to make this a bigger success than ever. I'm really optimistic about the Church."

Father O'Donnell and Sister Corde were only two of an estimated million pilgrims who passed through Philadelphia at some stage of the eight-day 41st International Eucharistic Congress. Most of

the serious participants came with some deep concern, some spiritual hunger etched on their faces and in their attitudes.

All were motivated by a deep hunger to know God better and to partake fully of his blessings.

Many also arrived with a need to un-

derstand how to satisfy the hunger of the poor and unfortunate for bread, for material aid, and for one-to-one relationships with sympathetic Christians.

Those who regularly confront oppression and prejudice came with a profound hunger for freedom and justice, a Christian approach to civil rights and social action.

A growing number expressed a hunger to be filled by the full power of the Holy Spirit and to exercise some of the many gifts He offers to committed Christians.

Others indicated their main hunger was to find those fundamental truths that all Christians can accept and use as an ecumenical basis to share not only fellowship, but the very Eucharist itself.

Husbands, wives and children entered the City of Brotherly Love with a compelling hunger to understand one another, and their mutual relationship with God through his Son, Jesus.

Dozens of ethnic and other special interest groups joined in the celebration because of their hunger to overcome factionalism and controversy and to find that

peace, "which is beyond all understanding," (Philippians 4:7), the inner calm which can lead directly to peace among Christian peoples.

Finally, all in Philadelphia hungered for a deep encounter with Jesus, the Bread of Life, who is present in every Eucharist and offers the only bridge between man and man, and between man and God.

As they moved through this week of prayer, celebration and study, many of the faces that were tense with these hungers relaxed into smiles of discovery and satisfaction. Jesus promised in Matthew 18:20, "Where two or three are gathered

in my name, there am I in their midst," and that promise came true for many of the pilgrims in Philadelphia. The story in the following pages dwells more on people than on events, more on the personal presence of Christ in individual lives than on abstract theology or ecclesiastical organization. Some of the pilgrims who tell their spiritual adventures are well-known; others are ordinary parishioners who may never again be mentioned in any book. But all show there is reason for optimism about the future of the Church. All are a living commentary on the truth of Jesus' statement in the Beatitudes, "Blest are they who hunger and thirst for holiness; they shall have their fill" (Matthew 5:6).

"When
you seek
me with
all your
heart..."

Hunger
for God

On the first page of his *Confessions*, St. Augustine wrote this prayer: "Thou hast made us for Thyself and our hearts are restless till they rest in Thee." These words may be an appropriate motto for the entire human race, because each of us experiences at one time or another a deep need to find ultimate meaning in life. Some seek this meaning in careers; others concentrate on a husband, wife or child; and still others pursue some man-made philosophy. But the satisfactions from these solutions are fleeting. A deep, instinctive hunger for a personal relationship with the Creator still remains and inevitably surfaces when career, family and philosophy fall short of our expectations. Our "restless hearts," as Augustine puts it, can only find peace in God Himself.

To satisfy the gnawing hunger for God, we must go to his house, sit at his table, and enjoy the living bread that He has made for us. But it's easy to get lost along the way, to become distracted by the cares and temptations of the world. Perseverance and singleness of purpose are prerequisites for finding our path to the banquet God has prepared. The Lord, speaking through the prophet Jeremiah, put it this way: "When you look for Me, you will find Me. Yes, when you seek Me with all your heart, you will find Me with you. . . ." (Jeremiah 29:13-14).

God's Son, Jesus, reaffirmed the need for such serious seeking in his parables and other teachings. He also made it clear that there is only one route to the Father's feast, only one way to satisfy the hunger of the heart for God. "I am the way . . . no one comes to the Father but through Me," Christ told his disciples (John 14:6). His words are as applicable to us and to the pilgrims who streamed in and out of the 41st International Eucharistic Congress in Philadelphia, as they were to his first-century followers.

TOURIST OR PILGRIM?

Architecturally speaking, the search to satisfy the hunger for God couldn't have begun in a more impressive setting than Philadelphia's Cathedral of Saints Peter and Paul, the site of the Solemn Opening Mass. Gold rosettes, reminiscent of the stars in the heavens, shone against rich blue panels in the lofty, coffered domed ceilings. Bronze chandeliers, weighing a half ton each, hung down like majestic planets to light the nave, where about two thousand worshipers gathered to celebrate the first Eucharist of the Congress on Sunday, August 1, 1976.

Many of the congregants were obviously interested in the spiritual dimensions of the Mass. One gray-haired woman, her head covered by a wispy black veil, moved her lips silently in prayer. Her fingers slipped lightly over her rosary beads, which she had wrapped tightly around one hand. Many other worshipers kept their heads bowed reverently as they clasped their hands quietly on their laps.

But there was another side to the celebration that would have delighted any tourist, a colorful, festive aspect that kept others in the Cathedral craning their necks from side to side. Prominent Philadelphians, such as Mayor Frank Rizzo, filed into the walnut pews and inspired priests, nuns and lay people to pop up periodically to catch flash bulb shots

with their Instamatics. Perhaps the greatest stir arose when Prince Rainier, Princess Grace of Monaco and their children filed into one of the front rows. "It's Grace Kelly, the princess!" one excited woman whispered, and all eyes around her turned to the stunning former actress who was wearing a snow-white turban and dress. One abbot near the front actually began to study the royal family with a pair of high-powered binoculars. Television crews, reporters and professional photographers in the audience also added to the excitement.

The near-carnival atmosphere changed to a quieter, more reverent kind of exuberance as the procession started down the middle aisle. The colors worn by the participants were dazzling. Many of the priests wore chasubles with the distinctive gold and green sprig of wheat decorating the front, to signify the bread of the Eucharist. Some of the cardinals and bishops wore tall, white mitres, or twin-pointed headdresses, signifying Old and New Testaments brought together in Christ. Others were adorned with striking bright red and purplish

birettas, zuchettos and cassocks. Members of the Knights of Columbus marched in with their swords drawn and colorful plumes trailing from their ornate military hats. Every race was represented in the procession, which was a testament to the incredible diversity of people who call themselves Roman Catholics.

Toward the end of the slowly moving line, as the huge choir and congregation sang "Crown Him with many crowns, . . ." His Eminence John Cardinal Krol,

the Archbishop of Philadelphia and Chairman of the Board of Governors of the Congress, came into view. Just behind him, in the position of honor, His Eminence James Cardinal Knox, the Papal Legate, strode majestically through the congregation, one of his hands holding an ornate crozier, or staff—symbol of his office as Shepherd—and the other hand blessing the crowd.

The concelebrating bishops and cardinals, who took seats together in pews near the altar, resembled waves of blanched wheat in their white mitres as they moved back and forth with the unfolding liturgy. Cardinal Knox, with his crozier planted firmly at his side, delivered a homily which set a Christ-centered tone for the entire congress. Quoting Pope Paul VI, he said, "To all these hungers of the human family, the Eucharistic Congress will offer, with confidence and loving faith, the only—the perfect—solution: Jesus Himself, Who said, 'I am the bread of life. He who comes to Me will never be hungry and he who believes in Me will never thirst.' "

The cardinal concluded by declaring, "As we examine each of these hungers, may we progressively put aside illusions and become convinced that Christ is the

solution to all difficulties. And if we ask why the world in its strife, tribulation and unhappiness, has not tried this solution, we may be obliged to ask ourselves: Have we Christians really tried this solution? Have we shown that this solution is effective in our lives? Only on the measure that we do so can we become a cogent sign to the world that 'Christ is the solution of all difficulties.' "

The Mass ended with the congregation taking Holy Communion as the choir sang a hymn, "Gift of Finest Wheat," which was composed especially for the congress by Omer Westendorf and Robert Kreutz.

Outside the Cathedral about two thousand people stood near the doors, unable to get inside because every seat had been taken. Some were disappointed, but most looked forward to the rest of the congress with a sense of hope that their spiritual hungers and the hungers of many others would be filled.

Sister Eileen Lynch, a teacher at St. Dominic Academy in Jersey City, came seeking "a closer union with Jesus, a renewal of faith, hope and love . . . a sharing with others and a caring for others . . . the joy of being together."

Brother Joseph Davis, executive director of the National Office of Black Catholics in Washington, expressed the hope that "many of the events that take place here would bring home to the Catholic people the real hungers that exist in the world, including poverty and the need for justice."

Joan Coakley of Manhattan confided, "I don't think anybody has it all straightened out. You can always learn more by seeking further knowledge of the Church."

Veronica Ryan of Devon, England, said, "You hear a lot about physical hunger, but I think people also want something more spiritual from life. I hope perhaps I can give something." Then she looked longingly toward the Cathedral

and sighed, "I would like to have been inside."

Bonnie Lea of Philadelphia indicated that she expected the Eucharistic services to give her "a better understanding of mankind and help me get closer to God and be able to get along better with other people in the world. I love the Catholic religion because it brings closeness to God, unity."

So, undergirding the pomp and elaborate liturgies, there were deep expressions of a grassroots faith, a hunger

in individuals to draw nearer to God. The rich interior of the Cathedral and the spectacular liturgical vestments were only outward symbols of a genuine inner exuberance.from hearts that had found, or were about to find, a deeper relationship with God. The depth of these spiritual experiences was revealed even more clearly later on Sunday afternoon as a Eucharistic parade began at Independence Hall. Thousands marched across town to Logan Circle and then up Benjamin Franklin Parkway in a candlelight procession to the Philadelphia Museum of Art.

Watching the parade from a sidewalk across from Independence Hall, a Filipino priest, Father Paul Cunanan, smiled slightly as one of scores of Marriage Encounter groups walked by, arm-in-arm, singing "They'll know we are Christians by our love!"

The 37-year-old Father Cunanan was quick to give his reasons for attending the congress. "I came here not as a tourist, but as a pilgrim," he said. "Becoming a Christian is an ongoing thing, a series of renewals. I believe we should all be searching for meaning, fulfillment, and relevance. And I know it's in Christ that we'll find this meaning for our lives."

Father Cunanan thinks that "the modern world is crumbling." He believes the answers to the problem of modern life lie in the Church, but he sees "a lot of division, a dichotomy in Catholic life. We

bread. You know, Jesus said we should not live by bread alone, but by every word that comes from the mouth of God."

The fervor of the Filipino father, who wore aviator glasses and a gray suit over his black shirt and clerical collar, had attracted the attention of several other bystanders. His visit to the Philadelphia congress, he explained, was a part of a four-week pilgrimage he was making with five other Filipino priests. They had visited Rome, Vienna, Zurich, Madrid, Paris, London and New York. He stressed his main hope had been that God would show him how to bring together his personal faith and his desire to be an effective social activist in the martial law regime of the Philippines.

"I've been a social activist in my country, and my exit visa was denied twice by the government," he confessed. "But on this pilgrimage, when I visited Paris, I also experienced a spiritual renewal. I visited the shrine of St. Therese, the Little Flower, and was impressed by her simplicity and purity. For the person who is pure inside, everything becomes pure. Goodness can be drawn out of every situation because the power of the Spirit of Christ drives you. I began to under-

say one thing and do another. There is too little integration of our physical and spiritual lives." Then he gestured toward a passing banner that proclaimed "Jesus, the Bread of Life" and observed, "The physical and spiritual life can be integrated in the Eucharist, and that's the message of this congress for me. Christ is the bread of life. That is what is most meaningful to me as a pilgrim here. I'm interested in the kind of bread that lasts—not just temporal but eternal

people, our weather, our natural resources—blessings that other nations don't always possess. I've been able to do a comparative study of our blessings on my pilgrimage, and I'm much more thankful for what we have. And I'm thinking about how we can exploit our strengths and talents. The East and West meet in the Philippines, and I think we have a mission there for the rest of Asia."

Part of Father Cunanan's social concern stems from the fact that he is the son of a farmer. He was born in the mountains south of Manila of a poorer family than many of his fellow priests. He knows what it is to do without, and this understanding has encouraged him to help organize economic cooperatives and establish a summer camp to train young men in Christian community leadership. "You can't solve these problems unless you do your own homework, and I'm being challenged to do more of my homework on this trip," he declared.

But his experience at the shrine of

stand how the spiritual and secular realities can be reconciled through a purity of intention, the motivation of love. Unless we grasp the reality of an intense love for other people, there can be no justice. I found I needed a new spirit which included Augustine's secularity, Paul's zeal and Therese's purity."

His contact with Christians from other nations in Philadelphia also was giving him a sense of perspective on his own Christian community at home. "We have the Spirit of Christ in the Philippines, but we don't know how to use it in the social realities," he explained. "We are person-oriented by nature, famous for our hospitality. We're always interested in the well-being of others. I'm beginning to see what blessings we have in our

St. Therese, and his insights in Philadelphia and elsewhere have given him an even deeper need to be certain that Jesus Christ is the integrating factor in all his endeavors. "Christ is the filter for everything we do," he said. "If we leave social reforms up to national leaders we'll be caught up in a personality cult. Any light we have will be stopped by these leaders, who are spiritually like opaque objects. They may be fine for national leadership, but they can't lead the entire world. Only Christ can do that because God's light of goodness, truth, freedom and justice passes through Him to us. He is the only transparent medium for God's love, which can integrate our bodies, minds and spirits."

When Father Cunanan returns to the Philippines, he will carry with him a better idea of how God wanted him to develop as a priest of God and servant to his people. "In my native language, Tagalog, we have a term, 'bayani santos,' " he said. "In English, that is translated 'heroic saint,' or 'saintly hero.' That is what I believe a Christian should be. It's not enough just to be an activist because you can be killed on the spot, and your work may end with you. Also, it's not enough to be an isolated saint, irrelevant to the needs of the community. We must have both a social conscience and an inner spiritual integration which transcends our national boundaries. We must be both activists and saints."

True to his words about acting on his faith, this thoughtful priest caught the eye of some of his compatriots who were marching behind one of the "hunger" banners in the parade, excused himself, and rushed off to join them. He thus added his own presence to the approximately fifty-thousand who were declaring by their participation that God in Christ is the answer to every human hunger. Father Paul Cunanan also caused his interviewer and several eavesdroppers to ponder more deeply the meaning of their own relationships with God.

As Father Cunanan's action indicated, there was a considerable amount of interaction between the bystanders and the participants in the parade. In fact, it was often hard to tell one from the other. One young man, walking along with his high school band, saw his parish priest in

the crowd and called out, "Hi, Father Dodd!" The scene could easily have been captured on a *Saturday Evening Post* cover by Norman Rockwell. Appropriately enough, many of Rockwell's works are on display in the Curtis Publishing House, which overlooked the parade route.

But the special spiritual dimension of the march was evident in the Jesus-centered banners and the songs like "Alleluia," which were popular among the Marriage Encounter couples. It was the Marriage Encounter groups, from such far-flung locations as Ireland, Canada and California, which gave the event its distinctive spiritual exuberance. They wore T-shirts with slogans like "Marriage Encounter is for Lovers," and encouraged

onlookers to join them with shouts such as, "I love you from Minnesota!" The Catholic couples who are involved in this movement to enhance marriage relationships titillated the interest of many in the crowd, who wondered how any long-married husband and wife could be hold-

ing hands and showing affection so enthusiastically in public.

Many priests and nuns who had
worked with the Marriage Encounter
groups strode along with their arms
around the couples. And a number of
bishops, not to be outdone, began to leave
their designated seats in a stand at the
Cathedral and mix with the crowds. One
of the bishops pulled out his camera and
started to take pictures of the people who
in turn, were taking pictures of him. Then
he and several of the other bishops posed
for shots with a number of the pilgrims. A
hotdog vendor moved among the bishops
and jokingly compared his blue and yellow umbrella with their purple robes. The
only people who seemed disturbed by the
interaction were the police and security
guards who were charged with the wel-
fare of those in the upper echelons of the
Church hierarchy.

As darkness fell on Philadelphia,
most of the marchers lit candles and in the
glow of the flames moved up toward the
museum where they heard Cardinal Krol
give a homily and Cardinal Knox, the

Papal Legate, deliver a benediction on
the day's activities. Quiet settled on the
marchers and bystanders, whose num-
bers had swelled to an estimated three
hundred thousand during the day. The

serenity of the candlelight had something
to do with the change in mood, but the
key factor was the exposed Blessed Sacrament, which had been placed on one of
the floats at the beginning of the
candlelight procession. The pilgrims in
Philadelphia seemed to realize that
somehow, whatever their spiritual
hunger, the presence of Christ in the
Eucharist contained the means of fulfillment. Many had started the day by taking Holy Communion in the Cathedral of
Saints Peter and Paul or in one of the
other Masses held throughout the city.
And with folded hands and bowed heads
they had walked away from their priests,
singing the words of the song written
especially for the congress: "You satisfy
the hungry heart with gift of finest wheat;
come give to us, O saving Lord, the bread
of life to eat." Those same words were
echoing through the minds of many of the

pilgrims as they turned thoughtfully toward their homes and hotels Sunday night. The message of the first day of the 41st International Eucharistic Congress was that the hunger for God can only be satisfied in a genuine encounter with his Son, Jesus Christ: Whether a person wishes to approach God for the first time, or, as Father Cunanan did, renew an old faith relationship, it is necessary to follow the Son to the Father.

The Scriptures are filled with the Good News that the universal longing or restlessness for God that St. Augustine knew could be satisfied by Christ. Perhaps John puts it best in the first chapter of his Gospel: "In the beginning was the Word; the Word was in God's presence, and the Word was God. . . . He was in the world, and through Him the

world was made, yet the world did not know who He was. To his own He came, yet his own did not accept Him. Any who did accept Him He empowered to become children of God."

Only when this basic hunger for God is satisfied can we move on to deal with the more specific hungers that plague the human family. Only when we have entered into a committed, powerful relationship with God through Christ can we deal in a completely effective way with individuals who desperately need our help. Many of the Philadelphia pilgrims who had experienced Christ's presence in the Eucharist seemed to recognize these truths as they looked forward to confronting another major human hunger—the hunger for bread.

Hunger
for Bread

Most Christians get a warm feeling when they drop a few dollars into a Sunday collection plate or contribute to some worthy charity. We tend to get a "Well, I've done my part!" feeling after such giving, but Jesus warned against this sort of attitude. Remember the time when He was watching the wealthy people put large contributions into the temple treasury, and the poor widow slipped through to put in her two small copper coins? Jesus called his disciples over and told them, "I want you to observe that this poor widow contributed more than all the others who donated to the treasury. They gave from their surplus wealth, but she gave from her want, all that she had to live on" (Mark 12:43-44).

The Lord encouraged giving until it hurts. He also stressed the importance of developing personal relationships because He knew they involved the most demanding contribution of all. It's one thing to give to a charity and then go about your own business. But it's quite another thing to pay a series of visits to a sick person; to spend hours counseling a distraught or confused friend; or to provide food for a beggar. This kind of individual action takes time and emotional energy, which we are often less willing to donate to others than our money.

Jesus made it clear that He expects this dedication of time and effort to needy individuals from those who follow Him. And Christ promised that when He comes in his glory, He will say, "You have my Father's blessing! Inherit the kingdom prepared for you from the creation of the world. For I was hungry and you gave me food, I was thirsty and you gave me drink, I was a stranger and you welcomed me, naked and you clothed me" (Matthew 25:31, 34,36).

This emphasis on the personal involvement of the Christian with the poor in body and mind was a constantly recurring theme at the Eucharistic Congress in Philadelphia. And the main symbol of this concern was a retiring, diminutive, 65-year-old Yugoslavian nun who has devoted her life to serving the poorest of the poor in Calcutta, India.

LIVING SAINTS

Wearing a simple white sari with a blue border and old leather sandals like those a certain Carpenter's mother might have worn, Mother Teresa of Calcutta smiled shyly at the thunderous standing ovation that greeted her. Hundreds of well-wishers and admirers, hoping for a touch or a word of assurance, had surrounded her constantly during the opening days of the Eucharistic congress. Her work with the Missionaries of Charity, an order she founded, has earned her the reputation of being a "living saint," and many Christians throughout the world believe she represents some of the greatest possibilities in expressing Christian love. Now the time had arrived for her major speech on the hunger of the poor, and thousands in the audience waited breathlessly for some word of spiritual wisdom that they could apply to their own lives.

When the applause had died down, the small nun, who walks and stands humbly, with a slight stoop, began by turning the attention of the crowd away from herself and toward another great Christian example: "Seven hundred and fifty years ago, St. Francis of Assisi made this prayer for himself and the people he taught to love God: 'Lord, make me a channel of Thy peace, that where there is hatred, I may bring love; that where there is wrong, I may bring the spirit of forgiveness; that where there is discord, I may bring harmony; that where there is error, I may bring truth; that where there is doubt, I may bring faith; that

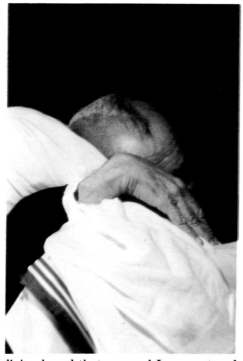

where there is despair, I may bring hope; that where there are shadows, I may bring light; that where there is sadness, I may bring joy. Lord, grant that I may seek rather to comfort, than to be comforted; to understand, than to be understood; to love, than to be loved. For it is by forgetting self that one finds; and it is by forgiving that one is forgiven; and it is by dying that one awakens to eternal life. Amen.' "

In clear, heartfelt tones that immediately tapped the deepest emotions of her listeners, Mother Teresa said, "God loved the world so much that He gave his son, Jesus. And Jesus Christ became one of us, like us, in all things except sin. He kept on saying, 'Love one another, as I have loved you.' And how did Christ love us? He made Himself the bread of life, a living bread that you and I may eat and live. He made Himself so small, so weak, just bread, to satisfy our hunger for God. . . . But Christ [also] had a [great desire] for your love and my love. To satisfy his hunger for our love, He made Himself the hungry one, the naked one, the homeless one, so that you and I may see Him, may touch Him, may know Him, may love Him, may serve Him. That is why I say that our sisters and brothers, the Missionaries of Charity, are not social workers. They are contemplatives right in the heart of the world. Their lives are [centered] in the Eucharist by touching Him in the appearance of bread, and then finding Him in the distressing disguise of the poor."

Her audience was deeply touched by these words and broke out in spontaneous applause. Her obvious sincerity, the deep aching she clearly felt for the unfortunate, was already moving many to tears. "When we come before Him, we will be judged on what we have been, what we have done to the poor. For He said, 'I was hungry, and you gave Me to eat. I was hungry not only for bread, but for that understanding love, to be wanted, to be known, to be somebody to somebody.' The poor do not need our sympathy and our pity. The poor need our love and compassion. They give us much more than we give to them."

Perhaps the greatest impact she made, though, was in telling the many poignant stories in her life, the concrete illustrations of what she and her sisters do on the filthy streets of Calcutta. "We went out in Calcutta and picked up four or five [people] in the street, and we took them to our home for the night. One of

one second, I reflected on looking at her, 'What would I have done if I were she?' My answer was that I would have tried to draw some attention to myself. I would have said, 'I am hungry, or I'm cold or I'm dying.' But she . . . she was so grateful, so beautiful in her giving. The poor are great people."

Waves of applause swept the Philadelphia Civic Center at these words, and more than one hard-bitten reporter could be seen weeping openly. As Mother Teresa returned to her story, listeners could not help but apply what she was saying to their own situation. "In Calcutta, we have had great difficulty with sugar. One little child of four years brought me a small bottle of sugar. He said, 'I will not eat sugar for three days. Give this to your children.' This little one loved with a great love. He deprived himself. He loved until it hurt.

"A few weeks before I came here, somebody came to our house in the evening and said, 'There is a Hindu family with eight children. They have not eaten for some time.' I took some rice and went

them was in very bad condition, and I told the sisters I would take care of her. I did for her all that love could do. As I put her in bed, she took hold of my hand, and there was such a wonderful smile on her face. She said only, 'Thank you,' and she died. She gave me much more than I gave her. She gave me her grateful love. For

straightaway there. I saw their hungry faces, their eyes shining with hunger. Their mother took the rice from my hands; she divided it in two and then went out. When she came back, I asked her, 'Where did you go? What did you do?' And she said, 'They are hungry also.' The next door neighbors were a Moslem family with as many children. She knew they were hungry. She was doing what Jesus does. She [gave] her love, the love of Christ, and shared with them. The faces

of those little ones . . . I knew they were suffering, I knew they were hungry. But when I left the room, their eyes were shining with joy because the mother and the children were able to share their love with others.

"Do we really know our poor? Do we really know the poor in our own house, in our own family? Maybe we are not hungry for a piece of bread. Maybe our children, our husband, our wife are not hungry, are not naked, are not homeless. But are you sure there is no one there who feels unwanted, unloved? Where are your old father and mother? Where are they?

"I visited a home, one of the best homes in England for old people. I've never seen so many beautiful things in a home. Yet there was not a single smile on the faces of those people. All those old people were looking toward the door. I asked the sister in charge, 'Why are they like that? Why are they not smiling? I'm so used to seeing smiles on people's faces.' She said, 'It's like that every day. They're always waiting for someone to come and visit them. The loneliness is eating them up. For days and days they keep on looking, but nobody turns up.' That unwantedness is great poverty."

Mother Teresa's intense involvement with those from every social class, those having almost every personal need imaginable became more and more evident as she spoke. "I saw a young boy with beautiful long hair sitting at night in the street," she recalled. "I said to him, 'You shouldn't be here. You should be with your parents. This is not the place for you to be sitting in this cold night.' He looked straight into my eyes and said, 'My mother doesn't want me because I have long hair.' That was all. I reflected for a second that it was quite possible that his mother was very busy with the hunger of India and Africa and all these places. She wanted to feed everybody except her own child. She did not know that the poverty of hunger was in her own home and she was the cause of that hunger. This is why I ask, do we really know our poor? Do we know how poor we are? For me, a nation that destroys the life of the unborn child, the child that has been created to live and love in the image of God, is very poor. The child is to be destroyed because [the parents] are afraid they cannot feed, cannot educate one more child. The child must die that they may live. This is very great poverty."

The response of the audience was particularly loud after these statements. The anti-abortion sentiment seemed to be one of the most pronounced attitudes among those attending the congress during the entire week of Eucharistic celebration. Then Mother Teresa returned to her predominant theme: "We must love the poor not by feeling pity, but because it is Jesus in the distressing disguise of the poor. They are our brothers and sisters. Those lepers, those. dying, those hungry, those naked—they are our Jesus. One of our sisters had just joined us. She had to go to a home for the dying, but before she went I said, 'You always have Mass, Holy Communion in the morning. You see with what tenderness, with what love Father touches the body of Christ. [You can be] sure it's the same body in the poor you will be touching. Give that same love, that same tenderness.' She went, and after three hours returned to my room and said, 'Mother, I've been touching the body of Christ for three hours.' Her face was shining with joy. I said, 'What did you do, sister?' She said, 'Just as we arrived, they brought a

man covered with maggots. For three hours, I have been touching the body of Christ.' She was a young sister who had understood that Jesus cannot deceive. He has said, 'I was sick and you took care of me.' "

Most of those who were listening to Mother Teresa so raptly were especially struck by her mixture of humility and humor. These qualities surfaced frequently in the closing moments of her address. "You pray for us, that we may not spoil God's work," she asked, prompting a burst of affirmative applause. "After reading the Gospels, I always have to smile at the people who say to me, 'You are spoiling the poor by giving them free [things].' I think no one has spoiled us more than God Himself because He

ation at her honesty. "I remember some professors came to our house. They asked, 'Tell us something, Mother, that will change our lives.' I said, 'Smile at each other.' Another ripple of laughter and applause indicated that her point was striking home. "One of them asked me, 'Are you married?' " More laughter. "And I said, 'Yes.' " Understanding applause. "I find it's sometimes very difficult to smile at Jesus: He can be very demanding."

The deafening applause that followed this comment showed that Mother Teresa's words weren't part of a speech to be given and forgotten. Pilgrims throughout the congress buzzed for days about what she had said. A group of Benedictine nuns from the Annunciation Priory in Bismarck, North Dakota, were particularly impressed by the Calcutta sister's talk.

One of these nuns, Sister Rita Miller, a physical therapist, said, "I take care of everyone, from children to grandmas who are one hundred years old. But I see so many people who come in with more

always gives to us freely, and I think it's good that at least one congregation spoils the poor, because everybody is spoiling the rich," she remarked with a smile. Laughter and applause arose from the audience.

"So let us look straight into our own families, for love begins at home," she concluded. "Do we really understand the poverty of Christ, the poverty in our own home? Sometimes I find it very difficult to smile at my sisters. It's much easier to smile at the people outside than to smile at your own, inside." The audience laughed again in amazement and appreci-

than just physical needs. It's too easy to get in a hurry and forget that it's not so much what we do physically for a person, but how well we listen to their inner needs. A patient may come in with a fractured leg after a car accident, and I'll have to exercise him every day to strengthen his leg muscles. During those sessions, which may last for twenty or thirty minutes, I'll help him move his leg through a complete range of motions. But the patient is constantly talking to me, asking me questions that deep down in his mind are troubling him. They may be questions about his spiritual life or his family, and he wants to know how I can assist him in some way.

"It really struck me when Mother Teresa mentioned how powerful a smile can be. She made me think, am I really taking enough time with people to give them a listening ear or a smile? And as a physical therapist, I was impressed by the story she told about one of her young sisters who touched that man with maggots for three hours. The young nun said she'd been touching the body of Christ, and I think that's what we have to re-

member in our lives. I keep thinking about that story, and I'm sure it's going to stick with me for the rest of my life."

One of Sister Rita's companions, a vivacious, white-haired parochial school teacher named Sister Carol Woida, had been leaning over listening to these re-

marks. Equally impressed by Mother Teresa, Sister Carol said, "I had quite an experience just before I came out here to Philadelphia. A lady called and said she would like a parish visitor to come to her home, and I said I'd be over there right away. That poor lady was so sick she couldn't walk. A heart condition had brought her down, and there was nothing

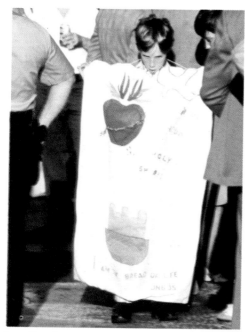

to eat in the house and nobody there to take care of her. I asked, 'When did you last eat?' She said, 'I don't even remember,' so I quickly got a meal ready for her. She said, 'You're an angel from heaven! I don't know what I would have done without you.' So for two weeks we brought her food, made her bed, cleaned the house and prayed with her. 'Just pray for me to get well enough so I can help myself again—that's all I want,' she said.

"At the congress I've heard so many things that encourage me in this kind of work. At the Mass for clergy and religious, John Cardinal Wright said in his homily that our attitude should be, 'Here am I! Lord! Send me!' That reaffirms the feelings I've had. When the Lord asks me to do his work, I must be willing to accept the task. And I have to agree with Mother Teresa when she said you get so much from helping the poor. Helping people like that sick lady is so rewarding for me."

Mother Teresa, the primary symbol of this kind of personal aid to the unfortunate, was an extremely difficult person to approach privately at the congress. Security guards and concerned associates frequently cordoned her off to keep her from being mobbed by the press and the grasping, spiritually-hungry crowds. But in an apparently providential convergence of circumstances, an interviewer for the *National Courier* happened to encounter the Calcutta nun for a few private moments after the Marian Liturgy in Philadelphia's Veterans Stadium.

"You're under a lot of pressure from the crowds here, Mother Teresa," the reporter said. "What's the main resource you have to keep your composure?"

"I have Holy Communion," she replied without hesitation. "Jesus is the bread of life, the key, the life, the everything. He is the very life of our life. If we didn't have the Holy Communion, if we didn't have the adoration, I don't think we would be able to do what we do. It's from the bread of life—seeing Christ in the appearance of the bread—that we can find Jesus in the distressing disguise of the poor."

Lord give
Bread
TO THOSE WHO HAV
HUNGER
give
OF
THEE
TO
THOSE
WHO
HAVE
Bread

"You mentioned in your speech to the congress that it's sometimes hard for you to smile at your sisters in the Missionaries of Charity—why exactly is that?"

"It's not spiritual problems," Mother Teresa replied. "It's human nature. Human nature is human nature everywhere. But it's so beautiful that we feel our weakness and our misery."

"What sort of difficulties do you have with your sisters?"

"I have no difficulties with the sisters—absolutely none!" she said emphatically. "The difficulties come from tiredness, I suppose. Like in your own family—don't you ever feel like that?" she asked, laughing.

"Oh, yes," the reporter answered, somewhat taken aback by having the questioning turned back on him.

"Same as our family," she said. "We have a family also."

The brief interchange ended as a burly plainclothes guard pushed in front of the interviewer and said gruffly, "I think we're going to have to leave now, Mother." The small woman was once again surrounded by protectors and whisked off into the night. But she left the impression of one with a quick wit and tremendous spiritual strength. It was also clear that her Christ-centered inner resources were constantly being tested by the inevitable fatigue that accompanied her demanding schedule and responsibilities.

Mother Teresa's devotion to the service of others, her desire to identify with them as she would with Christ Himself, was also reflected in the lives of a number of other dedicated Christians at the congress. Bob Froehlich, for example, founded the only American chapter of the Apostolate of Suffering in Albany, New York, after a 1969 visit to Guatemala. There he met the Most Rev. Constantino Luna, Bishop of Zacapa, and a member of the Silent Workers of the Cross. At the bishop's invitation, he founded the Apostolate.

The purpose of the seventy-member Apostolate is to provide a means for sick and suffering people—called "volunteers of suffering"—to help other handicapped people as a concrete expression of the redemptive message of Christ. Healthy workers at the Albany center are called "brothers and sisters," and that was Bob Froehlich's designation when he first started this ministry.

But several months before the congress, Bob noticed several lumps in his side as he lay in bed. The question that haunted him throughout that sleepless night was, "What if it happens to be cancer?" Recalling through tears the worries that had beset him, he said, "I told the Lord it couldn't be. After all, I had so much work to do at the center. And there were so many difficulties my workers were going to face in the future. How could it be that I would not be there?"

But it was cancer and Bob Froehlich himself became a "volunteer of suffering." He had to undergo surgery, and with the strain of chemotherapy treatments, he is often confined to a wheelchair. "It was only by the love of Christ that I had been interested in the handicapped," he said. "Did I want to suffer? Are you kidding? But after I found out that it was cancer, I said, 'Well, Lord, I

could help her show it to others.

"We Catholic Christians believe that the path Christ took to serve mankind is one through suffering. So there is a positive quality to suffering for us. It's impossible to explain sickness, sufferings and handicaps without the eyes of faith. [Pope] Paul has said that the suffering are the 'transparent images of Christ,' a continual reflection of that passion the Father always sees in the complete and total sacrifice of Christ."

After his operation, Bob says, he was particularly struck by his feeling of uselessness when he was forced to use a wheelchair. "I'm sure Christ wanted to carry the cross to Calvary, but He had to let someone else do it," he noted. "We [handicapped] give you the opportunity to show Christ to others. How do you think I felt when I saw my wife and two small sons struggling with the suitcases when we went to Lourdes? I tried to think about Veronica, who wiped the bloody face of Jesus. What anxiety did she have to go through before she pushed her way through the crowds to wipe the face of an [accused] criminal? So we say to our brothers and sisters who assist the handicapped, 'You've got to be the Veronica who is going to push through the crowd, in spite of being rebuffed.'

"It's still not easy for me. But if what I went through can help others come closer to Christ, and help others come to

guess You want me to know and understand how your sick feel.' I felt then that I could teach by example more than by preaching."

God immediately provided Bob with opportunities to be an example. When he entered a hospital to have his colon removed, one of the nurses inserted a tube the wrong way from his nose to his stomach. "By God's grace I was able to say, 'It's not your fault,'" he remembered. "And I meant it. I knew if I could show her Christ-like forgiveness, then I

49

grips with what they have. . . ." His voice trailed off as his mind went back over the months of pain he had experienced. "I'm not afraid to die," he finally said. "I've told God that. But my prayer has been that He'll let me be able to carry out the work I have to do." He would like to see the formation of other apostolates for the suffering, other havens for the unfortunate.

Mother Teresa emphasizes that "love begins at home," and she, Bob Froehlich and many other compassionate "living saints" are completely immersed in absolutely essential one-to-one relationships with the needy. But there are sometimes limits to what one individual can do for another. Oppressive governments and social structures may bear down on personal relationships and make it difficult, if not impossible, to express compassion effectively. It's at this point that the hunger for bread, the hunger to satisfy all the individual needs of the unfortunate, shades off into the hunger for freedom and justice.

Hunger for Freedom and Justice

It's been said that if the Good Samaritan happened upon a severely injured victim of highway bandits today, he would not only stop to give personal aid to the beaten man; he would also pressure governmental authorities to make the highway safer for travelers. The increasing involvement of government in our lives has made it necessary in many instances to take social and political action before we can act effectively as individuals to relieve the suffering and poverty of other individuals.

If one person wants to give a piece of bread or some medical aid to a needy brother or sister, he must be free to do his good deed. Class prejudices or official harrassment, though, may limit or completely stifle such intentions. If a capable, hard-working family head needs to apply for a better job to support his household, he should not be fettered by unfair business practices or unjust legal restrictions. Yet in many parts of the world innate human abilities are strangled and shackled by injustice.

From beginning to end, the Scriptures cry out for freedom and justice. Moses said in Deuteronomy 17:20, "Justice and justice alone shall be your aim, that you may have life and may possess the land which the Lord, your God, is giving you." And Jesus might as well have been talking to many of our own oppressive political leaders and to those who give tacit approval to unjust social systems when He declared, "Woe to you scribes and Pharisees, you frauds! You pay tithes on mint and herbs and seeds while neglecting the weightier matters of the law, justice and mercy and good faith. It is these you should have practiced, without neglecting the others" (Matthew 23:23).

It was typical of the realism of the Eucharistic Congress in Philadelphia that the need for freedom and justice throughout the world was given equal billing with the hunger for bread. Just as Mother Teresa of Calcutta became the rallying point for individual aid to the unfortunate, so another tiny figure, a five-foot-three-inch Brazilian archbishop, became a giant fiery symbol of Christian social and political action.

THE PADRE

Archbishop Helder Camara has become something of a legend as "the Apostle to the people" among Christians of the Third World because of the work he has done among the impoverished in his diocese of Recife-Olinda in Brazil. At first glance, though, he doesn't look exactly like the material of which legends are made. Short, balding, and thin with a wrinkled face that is frequently creased by a cherubic smile, he wears a plain black cassock and a simple wooden pectoral cross on a chain around his neck. No bishop's ring adorns his finger, nor is there any evidence of the usual reddish-purple piping on his garments to indicate his rank. He prefers to be called just "padre," or perhaps "Dom Helder."

Despite his simple appearance, Dom Helder has made an indelible mark on the Church during his sixty-seven years. The works he has sponsored to help the needy include literacy aids, a peasant worker self-help program, and an Action, Justice, Peace Crusade. He has received the Martin Luther King Prize for his efforts in social justice and was nominated for the Nobel Peace Prize in 1970. There was a tremendous anticipation as the "padre" walked up to the lectern at the Philadelphia Civic Center to deliver his first major address, and he didn't disappoint his listeners.

"My dear sisters, my dear brothers, I need your good will for my special English," he began, and from the warm cheering and applause, it was evident that his heavy Portuguese accent didn't matter one bit. "But with good will it is possible to understand and be understood. The biggest immorality is hate because hate is against love. Love is God."

With dramatic gestures, he launched immediately into a discussion of a major meeting of the Latin American hierarchy after Vatican II in Medellin, Colombia. Pope Paul VI himself opened the conference, and the conclusions of the Church officials were approved by the Holy See, Dom Helder emphasized. Three of the most important conclusions, he said, were a denunciation of "internal colonialism" in South America by which the rich keep millions in "a sub-human condition"; a declaration that injustices in

South America are "stratified in structures of oppression"; and finally, a decision to fight for a "liberating education" that would free the people from "sin and the consequences of sin, from selfishness and the consequences of selfishness.

"We need our personal conversion, it is true," he said. "Yes, you need to pray. I am afraid when I am facing persons that don't like to pray. It is so important to pray. But the personal conversion must open the eyes of all of us for the necessity of the social changes. We need the individual conversions, and without the personal conversions I don't believe in the Church," he declared, pounding on the podium as a crescendo of applause arose around the auditorium. "But we need to face the social injustices, the structures. And the great challenge is to change without hate and without violence. I don't believe in violence," he cried, gesturing dramatically as the cheering grew even louder. "My hands speak English very well!" he noted with a twinkle, provoking a wave of chuckles.

"Communism is not the solution, absolutely not!" he declared. "It is not sufficient to create certain material goods

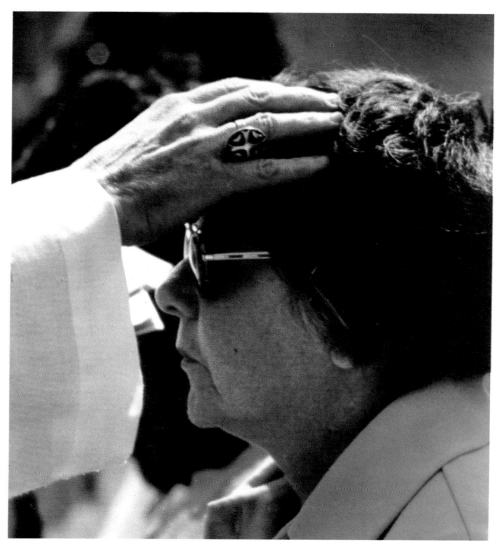

for people. Men also have hunger for liberty. It is essential. It is impossible for men to accept only material goods; there must also be a freedom to pray. When we have needy persons who are in hunger, though, we don't have the right to discuss, discuss! We must do what our words say!" the archbishop declared, rolling up the sleeves of his cassock to emphasize the importance of getting down to work. Then the crowd went wild when he said, "I ask your permission in

the name of the poor of the world to kiss the two hands of Mother Teresa."

Tears flowed freely as the frail, weathered archbishop walked across the speaker's platform, grasped the hands of the small Yugoslavian nun, and pressed them to his lips. It was perhaps the most moving moment of the entire congress. Before thousands of standing, cheering Christians, two saints who have devoted

their lives to the poor in different ways, and in opposite parts of the world, embraced. For a few brief seconds their love for the poor became one and united the hearts of all who witnessed the encounter.

On returning to the microphone, Dom Helder said, "We are denouncing the terrible injustices that at this moment are crushing more than two-thirds of mankind. We are being called subversive persons, Communists. It is terrible! There exists a great evil on our continent

and perhaps for the other continents because in fighting Communism and supporting the national security we are creating a new Nazism! Communism is not the solution, but in fighting Communism, is the only solution the creation of a new Nazism? I don't believe! I don't accept! We need to discover different ways, but not to fight a bad solution with another bad solution. There is no fight between justice and love. Oh, no! It is exactly because I love God, I love our brother Jesus Christ—it is exactly for

this reason that I am working for justice in the world."

Finally, rolling his R's dramatically, he said, "There is a wonderful Brazilian song that says, 'When one is dreaming alone, it is only a dream. When we are dreaming together, it is not only a dream! It is the beginning of reality!'"

Fascinated by the combination of

flamboyance and warmth in this man, a team of three *National Courier* interviewers sought him out in a rectory where he was staying in South Philadelphia. Dom Helder officiated at a 9:00 a.m. Mass with the local parish priest and then agreed to sit down for a rather lengthy chat before he flew back to Brazil that afternoon. The discussion ranged over a wide variety of topics, but the unifying

threads that ran through the talk were the small archbishop's intense personal faith and his deep compassion for the poor. On at least two occasions, tears welled up in his eyes as he recalled times when he lacked the means to give to a needy suppliant. Throughout the conversation, he grasped his interviewer's arms, punched them gently and gestured theatrically to make his points. Here are some of the highlights:

Q. "Could you tell us something about your own faith, your own personal spiritual life?"

A. "All of us need to have faith, a great faith when we are trying to work, because it is not so easy. Sometimes we meet misjudgments and obstacles when we [deal with] mankind in the very poor conditions. It is very important for me to have inspiration, deep inspiration. Fortunately, the world is receiving the presence of the Holy Spirit more and more."

Q. "How?"

A. "Jesus Christ and the Father Himself sent the Holy Spirit to help mankind. For instance, when I travel on international invitations, I meet more and more groups—minorities inside all countries, all races, all religions—who have determined to create a more human world. For me, it is not the work of man, not the work of a group. For me, it is the inspiration of the Holy Ghost. God is always demanding our collaboration. I am thankful that the Father only began the creation and that He needs our collabora-

tion, even though we are so weak. It is a mystery that He uses my hands. We are one with Christ since our baptism, and it is wonderful that our presence—the presence of Christians—is really the presence of Christ. Without the collab-

oration of the Holy Spirit, that is impossible.

"I believe in synchronizing the work of different groups of good will. There are so many persons of good will inside mankind, and I am so happy with the inspiration of our International Eucharistic Congress. It is wonderful for me. We have been invited to glorify the Holy Sac-

rament, but at the same time to think about the different hungers. We don't have the right to separate religion and life, evangelization and humanization. I don't believe in separating social action from faith and prayer. If you are only praying, [remember] Christ said it is not

sufficient to say, 'My Lord, my Lord!' Those are the words of Christ!"

Q. "How do you personally increase the power of the Holy Spirit in your own life?"

A. "With some persons, it is almost impossible to awake and then to sleep again. For me, it is very easy. During the day we are emptied by our people; persons are pulling me here and there; there are many demands on my time. I must receive many, many persons, above all, the poor. Sometimes I don't have . . . because they ask impossible things, I don't have the possibility of helping them. Sometimes they have requirements that I can't meet. For me, all persons are brothers and sisters, and it is not so easy when we receive persons without the possibility of giving something. But if the person discovers that we are suffering because we don't have the possibility of helping, it is wonderful for him. It is wonderful.

"[In these situations] we must keep remembering we are one with Christ, so I profit because of what God gives me every morning. I am awake at two in the morning. Sometimes I am tired physically, but man has not only physical rest. We also have spiritual rest. When we are talking to the Father, it is so easy to renew our unity with Christ. So I usually go to sleep at ten-thirty at night, and I awake at two in the morning and read my breviary and pray. When we try to talk with human beings, sometimes it is not so easy because of the problems of language. We may have to use sign language to be understood. But with God there are no

they awaken, find it is impossible to sleep again. But for me it is very easy. Then at 5:00 a.m., my day begins!"

Q. "Do you spend any time in praise and thanksgiving to God?"

A. "My spiritual rest in the morning is preparation for the Mass. And then the Mass covers my whole day, the beautiful scenes made by God's grace or by man, the co-creator. I was walking down a road looking at the sky and the sun, which were created directly by God, the Father. But then an airplane passed. Yes, it is also created, but this time it is the work of the co-creator, who receives his power from God. It is wonderful. All these things I see give me an opportunity to offer up [thanks], to continue the Mass. All of life is consecrated, all is holiness.

"For instance, this table once was a tree created by God. But also we have here the work of man, the co-creator. For me, it is wonderful because it has a wholeness in God and man. We may be in the Church or out of the Church, but we are never out of God. Inside Christ, we are one . . . Ah, I am dreaming of a world without divisions, without wars, without

problems. God is even able to understand my English. It is a time of spiritual rest for me because God is not only a distant Father, but a Father living inside us. Sometimes we say, 'Come in Holy Spirit! Come on!' We invite the Holy Spirit in, to be with us. As I pray, I like to remember the last day I was living. For instance, this next morning I will remember that I was with you now. You are working for the mass media, for the press. It will be easy for me to remember you, and you, and you. But I will pray not only for you personally, but for all the persons who work for the mass media. Also during the day I will meet priests, sisters, and perhaps a mother with her children. I will pray for them and, above all, for peace in the world, for more understanding among the different countries.

"Normally, I am up from two to four in the morning, and then from four to five, I sleep. I know that some people, after

hate, without races, with all created as brothers and sisters. But I know these are perhaps dreams, dreams, dreams."

Q. "Tell us about your experiences with some of the poor people in the United States."

A. "You have wonderful workers in this country. I have been with some minorities inside this country, such as the native Americans and the Hispanic people, and I have seen different pockets of poverty. Some days before the congress, I was visiting Los Angeles for a meeting on this very, very serious problem of the so-called illegal aliens. You know, the founding fathers of your country, the first settlers, were illegals too. They didn't have papers to show the native Indians. When the so-called illegals arrive today, it is not as tourists, not to visit the country. It is because the conditions in our countries are so bad. We all have a certain responsibility for the bad conditions that have created more and more arrivals of these so-called illegal persons. I can speak to you in this manner because I am not really a foreign man. I am your brother."

Q. "We've heard you have certain threats against your life back in Brazil because of your work with the poor. What about that?"

A. "It's not always easy for me to speak about myself. But a great part of my life is an effort at helping people. Many persons, though, don't really have an opportunity because they are so poor. It may be the problem of age, or the absence of health. So I receive these poor people.

"Once, one of my poor people was killed. I passed by on a street and saw him on the ground. The owner of a gasoline station had shot him because he was afraid the man might steal from him or assassinate him. Later that evening, two other poor people came to me and said, 'Do you know him, the man who was killed?' and I said, 'Yes.' They said he had received money and was told to come to me every day for help. Then, when a day arrived that I was not able to help him, he was supposed to create a disturbance and then get me during the confusion. It was a pretext, very intelligent. And an announcement would then be published that 'Camara was killed by the poor. He had not helped the poor, so the poor killed him.' I asked the two men who told me

why they didn't tell me this before, and they said they didn't have the courage.

"On another occasion, perhaps eight months ago, I arrived home late in the evening, and it was raining very hard. I met a poor man I knew, and he was completely drunk. 'You promised me you would not drink!' I said. 'Your health is not good!' He said, 'You are my father, my father, my dear father! They—they—they want me to kill you! I was here twice for that, but I didn't have the courage.' They promised him money, but evidently we are in the hands of God. I don't have too many hairs, but none of them will be cut without the permission of the Father. For me, to be killed is not a personal decision."

Q. "Who is trying to do this to you?"
A. "I prefer not to say who it is. Some persons do not approve my line of work. In my country—and not only my country—when we help the poor with food, clothes, medicine and in light of the Gospel we try to support human rights, justice and freedom, we are immediately judged as subversive persons, as Communists.

"Once, I presented a question to a very important person [who was] my friend: 'Why do you think I am a subversive person, a Communist?' I asked. He said, "It is very easy to understand. You know that it is easier, faster to open the eyes of the people than to do the basic reforms. You are trying to open the eyes of the people without the possibility at the same time of effecting the basic reforms. You are a subversive person because only the Communists are able to profit from this situation. You are helping the Communists!'

"I answered, 'You have the impression I am working very fast. But Latin America has been waiting four and a half centuries. Asia and Africa have been waiting millions of years. And you think I am a subversive man. The *situation* is subversive! At the moment, my people don't know how to hate. But you are teaching them! I am always hearing that we need to prepare the cake before we distribute it. But [you] are preparing it and eating it too!"

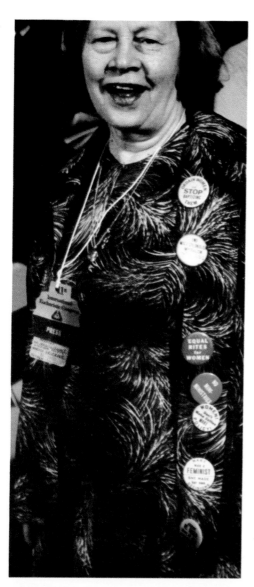

"But I am hopeful. The day we discover liaisons among more minorities, races, persons of good will, I am sure we will construct a different world."

Although Dom Helder Camara is in constant confrontation with government authorities, other pilgrims at the congress revealed more sanguine attitudes toward their political system. For example, Catherine Norton, a public school teacher for twenty-five years who lives in Cranston, Rhode Island, had attended Eucharistic Congresses in Munich, Bombay, Bogota and Melbourne with her twin sister Claire. One reason she came to Philadelphia is that this congress "fosters the ideals of patriotism and has intensified my love of country," she explained. "You know, we cannot love God without loving our country. I could not have attended the other four congresses had I not lived, worked and been educated in the United States. All these meetings have intensified my love for people throughout the world, but this year's congress has increased my love, appreciation and hope for the country and the Catholic Church. For a while I was losing hope in our country. Although I knew there were dark days, I knew also that

67

events like this congress would follow to confirm my convictions [that] this nation would emerge again as a world leader of Christ's followers."

Dom Helder Camara, who has expressed tremendous admiration and hope for the United States as a leader in the international struggle for freedom and justice, could probably agree with many of Catherine Norton's observations. But he is also a great believer in vigilance, in not becoming complacent and overlooking the "pockets of poverty," as he calls them, among our Appalachian whites and Southern California migrant farm workers. Of course, Jesus Himself also frequently warned the more fortunate who enjoyed many of God's blessings. In response to a question from Peter, He declared, "When much has been given a man, much will be required of him. More will be asked of a man to whom more has been entrusted" (Luke 12:48). If Dom Helder's words and experiences are at all prophetic, the same might be said of the affluent social classes and nations of our own day.

Hunger
for the Spirit

He may be called Paraclete, Counselor, Comforter, Spirit of God, or Spirit or Christ. Whatever the name, He is God's Presence among us, constantly ready to lead, respond, and minister to our every need.

Of course, to tap the full potential of the Holy Spirit's power in our lives, there are certain requirements on our part. We must be obedient to God by following without reservation his Son, Jesus Christ. We must *ask* the Spirit to take complete control of our lives, to fill us with his peace and supernatural energy. If we are willing to release the reins of our life to the Spirit's care, there will be no bounds to the blessings, the gifts, the fruits that only He can provide.

St. Paul understood the tremendous power of the Spirit as well as any man. He encouraged the Christians at Ephesus to become mature in the Spirit so they could realize their full potential as apostles, prophets, evangelists, pastors and teachers and thus "build up the body of Christ" in roles of service (Ephesians 4:11).

Writing to the church in Galatia, he stressed another dimension of God's Presence as Paraclete—the inner benefits we derive as obedient servants of Christ. ". . . The fruit of the Spirit is love, joy, peace, patient endurance, kindness, generosity, faith, mildness and chastity," Paul declared (Galatians 5:22-23). With the Holy Spirit guiding us both internally and externally in the affairs of daily life, we'll find ourselves being drawn closer to God the Father and being conformed more and more to the image of the Son.

It seems appropriate that the consideration of the Spirit in our lives was highlighted at the mid-point of the congress because one of his main functions is to bind all together, man with man, and man with God. Only when we are one with the Paraclete can we say with St. Paul, "The Spirit Himself gives witness with our spirit that we are children of God" (Romans 8:16).

COME, HOLY SPIRIT

Whenever we discuss God's work in the world, the presence of the Holy Spirit must always be implied, for the Spirit is the active, comforting hand of the Father and the Son in our midst. But on some occasions and in some movements, the work of the Spirit becomes especially obvious and intense. One of the best summaries of the striking work of this presence in the contemporary Roman Catholic Church came from Father Fred Bellotti, a young priest with a short beard who was ordained in 1972 and assigned to St. Joseph's Parish in Grand Junction, Colorado.

"Through the charismatic renewal the Spirit is teaching us about baptism in the Holy Spirit and the gifts of the Spirit for healing the body of Christ," Father Bellotti said emphatically.

"Through Marriage Encounter, the Spirit is renewing family life by renewing the couples and the priests in their relationship to each other.

"Through Cursillo the Spirit is giving a 'little course in Christianity' aimed at personal conversion and life in the community.

"Through the Better World Movement, the Spirit is calling Christians to love the merciful heart of Jesus.

"Through the Legion of Mary, the Spirit has always called people to serve others through the spiritual and corporal works of mercy."

There are, of course, many other focal points for the work of the Paraclete in our own day, but Father Bellotti put his finger on some of the most prominent.

We'll devote some time to Marriage Encounter and Cursillo in other contexts, but now let's turn our attention to the grassroots spiritual fire that is sweeping through many Catholic parishes—the charismatic renewal movement.

The recognized leader of the charismatic renewal movement in Roman Catholicism is Leon Joseph Cardinal Suenens, Archbishop of Malines-

Brussels and Primate of Belgium. Characteristically, he opened one of his main speeches at the congress by leading the audience in singing, "Come Holy Spirit . . . come with thy grace and heavenly aid, to fill our hearts which Thou hast made. . . ."

His listeners joined in with gusto and then waited expectantly for this high church official to share his spiritual insights with them. "Today, we will ask the

Holy Spirit to show us his presence," he declared in a precise Flemish accent. "Many things change in the Church, but one thing never changes: The Lord took bread and wine and said, 'This is my body and blood . . . this do in memory of Me. We have been doing this through twenty

centuries of fidelity. I believe Jesus Christ Himself is presiding at this congress. Jesus is more anxious than we are to be one with us in the mystery of the Eucharist," he said, always bringing the attention of his listeners back to the importance of the Holy Communion in their faith and in their celebrations at the congress.

The cardinal's presence on the podium was enhanced by his striking bright red cassock and the red zucchetto that crowned his steel-gray hair. But the real power in his message seemed to emanate from within, from a primary emphasis on Jesus Christ: "The Holy Spirit was given to actualize the presence of the Lord. Once you meet Jesus as a living reality, your life changes at once. The power of the Spirit makes Jesus alive now. We are not living by an abstraction, but by a Son with a mother. The Gospel is a letter written by the Lord to you. There is some line, some word for you, and the Holy Spirit will enliven that word. We must listen very carefully to the voice of

the Lord. It's not that the Lord is not speaking, but there is too much noise in the world. We have to make silence, listen to the Spirit."

In the hope of getting a more intimate view of the deep spirituality of this man, a *National Courier* team contacted one of his associates at his hotel in Philadelphia and arranged an interview. Sitting with the cardinal in a limousine

that was speeding him to the Philadelphia airport, the interviewers listened intently as the 72-year-old prelate described his spiritual journeys.

"When I opted for the priesthood as a boy, I was struck with the idea of eternity," he began. "I had an idea you had to

do something worthwhile for eternity, and the best way was to prepare other people for their eternity. I wanted to bring the Gospel, the good news to them. I was also attracted by the Holy Trinity, and especially by the Holy Spirit. In fact, when I became a bishop in 1945, I chose the motto, 'In the Holy Spirit.' I believe that everybody is converted five times or more, and I discovered the Holy Spirit more and more, until one day in 1973 I encountered the charismatic renewal in the United States. For me, that was an important moment. It was not a peak experience, but rather a release of the Spirit [in me]. I gained the courage to speak more freely about the Spirit, to let Him speak in me and make me more instrumental."

This greater sense of freedom, he explained, affected his entire life. "There was a sort of freedom in celebrating Mass. There was an order of liturgy you had to follow, and I tried to do it in the correct way, but there was more freedom in improvisation, more freedom to let the Spirit do his own work. There is also a courage to speak about the Lord when you meet people who apparently don't seem hungry. Giving food to somebody who is not hungry—or at least doesn't appear hungry—asks some sort of effort."

Changes also occurred in Cardinal Suenens' personal prayer and worship life. "The charismatic renewal stresses adoration with the Lord, a continuity in

prayer, and freer ways of praying. I have a prayer group at my home with intimate people around me. There are about ten people—those who work with me, my lay people, staff secretary—and we meet once a week. We read Scripture, share, give testimonies of what happened the last week, including answers to prayer. It's very spontaneous, and the meetings last about an hour and a half.

"We also have a little Eucharistic celebration in my own house once or twice a month, and we celebrate there also in a more free way. People intervene more [than is usual in a Mass], and speak in tongues when they wish it. Although people [at Mass] normally just listen to a homily, we let them react. They may say, 'I am touched by this! It appeals to me!' If you want to make something known, that

is the practical way to do it. These Masses may last two and a half hours. Also, once or twice a month, I invite priests and nuns—some Flemish speaking, some French speaking, some English speaking—from Brussels with the intention of making [what I am doing] known."

The cardinal, who also prays in tongues himself, believes that one of the main purposes of this kind of communication is to "let your conscious and subconscious come out and express to the Lord your adoration."

His increased awareness of the Holy Spirit in his life has also enhanced his relationship with Jesus. "Jesus was always, of course, the reason of my life," he said. "Otherwise, I should not have chosen the priesthood. But I [have developed] more the feeling that He is really a person you meet, just like we meet each other. He is more real when two or three are gathered in his name. For example, when I spoke here recently, I felt very strongly the words of the Lord on Holy Thursday when He said he desired to take that last meal [with his disciples]. He has been presiding at this congress in a more real way than we are. It is not Cardinal Krol or myself, but Jesus. That sort of vision, or consciousness, or awareness is what I mean. I can't say [my recent experience with the Holy Spirit] makes a revolution, but it makes a difference."

One way the Spirit makes a difference is in his approach to the Bible. "In reading the Scripture, [I have] more openness to the Spirit; I listen [more] to what He is saying through those words of Scripture. You can read those words a hundred times, and then in one moment they will say something."

Cardinal Suenens has also noticed the development of the gifts of the Spirit, but with certain reservations. "As for

prophecy in the sense of speaking about the future, no. But [I do see] people letting themselves go under the impulses of the Holy Spirit to speak a word of consolation and exhortation. I see people doing that more, and I think we have to believe in the working of the Holy Spirit in that way."

In his own personal ministry as a bishop, a shepherd over a spiritual flock, there has also been a transformation. "My definition of being a bishop is still the same, but my way of living has changed, yes. I will pray much more easily for a sick priest during a visit. I not only say I'm going to pray for you, but I'll do it on the spot. My own secretary and I will pray, lay hands on the sick, ask God's blessing for him. I wouldn't have done that before."

As a result of such prayer, he said, "I have had different people testify to me that they were innerly healed. For instance—and I believe it—I have two or three examples of persons very near to me who told me they received the grace of healing recently. Although I believe in such healing, that doesn't mean we shouldn't use human medicine or things like that. But I believe, essentially, that prayer is the source, the key. The Lord

said when you pray in faith He will listen to your prayer. Of course that doesn't mean if you ask for a certain thing, He will give just that. He may give another, better thing for you. I know God loves me, and that is enough. I have faith, not that I will obtain exactly what I am asking for, but that God will answer my prayers in his way. I have faith in that. The people I have seen healed have not been healed immediately, but after a while. But I cannot give any more personal information about that."

During the official meetings and liturgies of the congress, Cardinal Suenens said he was "surprised and joyed to see different cardinals opening themselves more and more [to the charismatic renewal]. It's new as far as the charismatic movement is concerned. The Spirit is not new, but the accent on the Holy Spirit working through the gifts and so on, is new."

Asked whether Pope Paul VI has had such a charismatic experience himself, the cardinal replied, "I don't know anything about that. But the pope has always been impressed by the Holy Spirit. Also, it was very striking, the letter he wrote for Pentecost about the joy in the Spirit. It couldn't have been better for us. I feel the charismatic movement in the Church is growing, though I can't speak for all the world. I see something coming, like springtime in February or March. You don't see the flowers yet, but I believe . . . generally the hierarchy is in favor. We have to avoid overstressing the Holy Spirit and denying human collaboration, though. The Holy Spirit is not working out of the blue. He is working with you and me, with your talent, your own personality."

The Belgian prelate also believes strongly that the current movements of the Spirit have profound implications for ecumenism. He recalled a spiritual insight he had when he and Dr. Michael Ramsey, the former Archbishop of Canterbury, sat down for a conversation at Malines. The cardinal, who referred to this incident in his book, *A New Pentecost* (Seabury Press, New York, 1975), suggested that they open the Gospel and "ask a word of the Lord." The verse that caught their eye was John 20:26: "Despite the locked doors, Jesus came and stood before them. 'Peace be with you,' he said."

"The word was that in spite of the fact that the doors were still closed, Jesus was in the midst of them saying, 'Peace be with you,'" Cardinal Suenens explained. "We know the doors are still closed, but yes, the windows are open and there is a key in the door. I am very engaged in ecumenical dialogues and am very open to go along that line. My good friend, Bishop John Allin, the presiding bishop of the American Episcopal Church, came by [the other night] just to say hello. He is a very nice man, and I prayed with him. That, for me, is a very important aspect

of the charismatic renewal. If we can pray together and meet together, that's a great step forward. It [the charismatic renewal] can move across the different Christian denominations."

Much of the enthusiasm and freedom that Cardinal Suenens had expressed became reality during the charismatic renewal Mass at Veterans Stadium. The tone for the celebration became evident during the procession, as some of the

priests and bishops, as well as thousands in the crowd, raised their hands to the heavens in praise of God. There was "singing in the Spirit," or in tongues, and much embracing and touching. One bishop was wheeled out in a wheelchair to the edge of the field, and several of his fellow clergymen walked over to hug him.

As the Holy Eucharist was carried in baskets around the field, it seemed that almost everyone present—priests, bishops, laity—had lifted their arms, palms upward, to the sky. "He's Lord. Let's expect miracles right here tonight. Surrender your life!" a voice said over the loudspeaker. "Tonight He calls us to surrender to Him completely, to accept Him as our Lord and our Savior, to turn away from sin and selfishness, to accept his love. He is Lord, He is Lord, He is risen from the dead, He is Lord."

Many of the congregants sang "He is Lord!" over and over as they waited in line in the aisles to partake of Communion.

There were also words uttered that were accepted by many as prophetic, as coming directly from God through the mouth of the speaker: "My beloved children, depend on Me, touch Me. You can trust Me, my children. My blood will feed you. My Eucharist will feed you . . . Look around you, my people. I am the bread of life, and my people are starving . . . I hunger for your love. My healing power is here. I am healing arthritis, the spine, the left knee. . . . My beloved sons [elders of the church], you who bring my body and my blood, I love you. Trust in my love. I know your loneliness, I know your frustration. Lean on Me. Some of you have sorrows in your relationships, in your relationship with Me. You must live for my sheep. You are al-

ways the shepherd, comforting the people. Trust in my power, in the power of my Spirit. Repent . . . turn to Me now for I love you . . . respond to my love. Lean on Me."

As the Mass drew to a close, thousands of worshipers, including countless nuns, were holding hands and swaying from side to side, singing in the Spirit, and then offering applause to the Lord. The spiritual enthusiasm which culminated in this Mass was also evident in charismatic "workshops" and other meetings at various stages of the congress activities.

The most striking feature in these smaller charismatic meetings was the freedom in giving personal testimonies. One young man, speaking extemporaneously before a room filled with several hundred people, many of whom were sitting in the aisles, recalled how his "reconversion" had begun during a conversation with his dying grandfather. The grandfather, in a thick Italian accent, told him, "I'm going to be working in heaven with the Lord, and you'll be working here with the Lord." The young man, who described his religion in those days as "dry and routine" said he didn't know what the old man was talking about. But after his grandfather's death, he felt more drawn to acquaintances who had undergone a genuine Christian experience. Finally, he said, the Holy Spirit spoke to him through another young Christian, and he made a permanent commitment of his life to Christ.

A married couple testified they had been baptized into Catholicism but found Jesus in a personal way when they got older. The husband explained, "I felt the Lord had His arms around my shoulders. It was a good feeling, and I began to experience an inner peace. We [he and his wife] prayed together, got into the Word, and our marriage was strengthened. We were changed by the Lord's love."

Those in the audience applauded after every talk and seemed to be acknowledging that the Spirit of God was not only moving in the large meetings of the congress, but in these individual lives as well.

The Holy Spirit works in varied ways, both to bring about initial commitments to Christ and to rejuvenate convictions that have grown stale and meaningless. But without exception, individual Christians at the congress, from Leon Cardinal Suenens to the youngest, most inexperienced lay person, indicated that their thrilling encounters with God involved some decision, some action on their own part. The Bible says unequivocally in James 4:8, "Draw close to God, and He will draw close to you." There is movement, initiative on both sides; we are expected to open our hearts and minds and receive in faith that grace which God so freely offers. Spiritual refreshment and power await those who respond honestly to that gracious invitation in Revelation 22:17: "The Spirit and the Bride say, 'Come!' Let him who hears answer, 'Come!' Let him who is thirsty come forward; let all who desire it accept the gift of life-giving water."

Hunger for Truth

Christians have embarked on a great search in the past few years in an effort to discover a common point of reference, a single great truth that will bind them together and enable them to commune as one. There have been many high-level conferences at which leaders of the various Christian traditions, especially the Catholics and Protestants, have explored their differences in theology and church tradition, and attempted to reach some common ground.

These efforts have sometimes fallen short of their goals, but most participants acknowledge that progress has been made. There is still deep pain among individual Christians who long for that day when they can enjoy full fellowship with every Christian brother and sister, but the pain is easing.

St. Paul set the ultimate ideal before us when he wrote in Galatians 3:27-28, "All of you who have been baptized into Christ have clothed yourselves with Him. There does not exist among you Jew or Greek, slave or freeman, male or female. All are one in Christ Jesus." Despite our recent progress, we are still far from this ideal. As a result, there is a lack of freedom in our interactions with one another. And where there is a lack of freedom, there are limits to the ways that we can express our love.

Jesus placed the highest value on the expression of love when he told his disciples in John 13:35, "This is how all will know you for my disciples: your love for one another." Perhaps this divine love for one another is the key, the primary teaching He wants us to rely on today as we struggle with the knotty theological and ecclesiastical issues of ecumenism. The teachings of Christ about love always seems to flow naturally into a truth that tends to bind believers together, rather than separate them. Or as the Lord Himself put it, "If you live according to my teaching, you are truly my disciples; then you will know the truth, and the truth will set you free" (John 8:31-32).

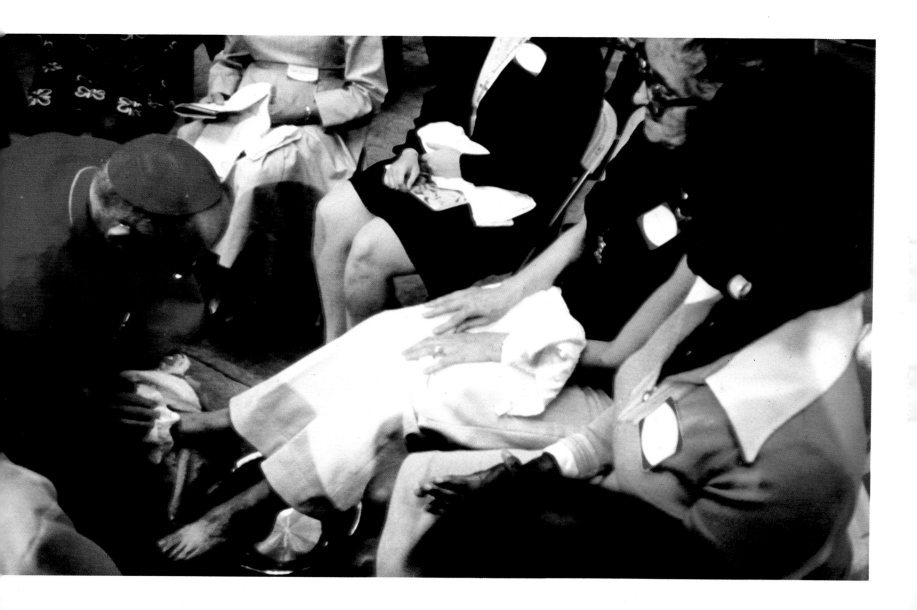

A LOVER'S QUARREL

The central dancer, dressed in a dazzling white robe, moved gracefully across the stage as the other dancers, wearing more ordinary robes, moved around him in adoration. The audience watching this presentation saw more than just some excellent choreography by the Germantown Dance Theatre. They saw the initial unity of Jesus and the apostles, and they also watched the disintegration of this unity after Judas turned traitor. But then other dancers, dressed in costumes of the many different Christian heritages, appeared in the background. They stayed separate for a time, then whirled together, holding hands and embracing one another in the finale. It was a beautiful symbolic representation of a major goal that the congress was helping to promote—greater ecumenical understanding.

As a huge choir led the audience in singing "Crown Him with many crowns, the Lamb upon his throne, . . ." a grandmother from the St. Francis Xavier

church in Brunswick, Georgia, Mrs. Mary Lenz, brushed away a tear that was trickling from her eye.

"Isn't that terrible! I'm crying!" she exclaimed to a stranger sitting next to her.

"Not at all," the man replied, blinking away his own tears.

Then Mrs. Lenz turned her attention back to the dais where one of her favorite Church figures, Archbishop Fulton J. Sheen, was about to speak. Neither she nor any one else was disappointed. Wearing his purple robes and zucchetto, or skull cap, he was by far the most strikingly-attired cleric on the speakers' platform, but he was not about to take

himself that seriously. Looking around at the more sedately dressed non-Catholic religious leaders behind him, he quipped, "I'm the only holy show here!"

The warm laughter from the audience launched one of the best-received talks of the congress, as the archbishop swept back and forth on the platform, disdaining the use of the lectern. At the outset, he continued to poke fun at himself. For example, he recalled one time when he had worn his red cassock into a restaurant to order graham crackers and milk for some other clergymen who wanted something to eat before they went to bed. The waitress took one look at him and cracked, "And how about you, cock robin? What will *you* have?"

With his audience entirely at ease, he moved into a discussion of what he considered the main ecumenical problems facing the different Christian denominations. "The problem is only a lover's quarrel," he said. "Husbands and wives don't fight about their love for one another. And we are agreed on one thing, too—our deep and profound love for Christ."

Mary Lenz, listening intently to Bishop Sheen's every word, exclaimed, "Isn't that beautiful!"

The archbishop made some of his most telling points when he began to speak by parable and analogy: "I believe that the pluralism of views begins to merge into unity when the Cross becomes the center of a study of the Eucharist. . . . There are hints everywhere in Scripture that the circle of Christ's Truth is best seen when refracted through his death. . . . So much emphasis has been

given to the life-giving side of the Eucharist that we forget its death-incorporating aspect. Are not all the metabolic processes of nature linked into the anabolic and catabolic? St. John speaks of its anabolic character; St. Paul and the words of the Last Supper dwell on the catabolic side.

"First, let's look at the anabolic, or life-giving side. If the sunlight, the moisture, the chemicals in the earth could speak, they would say to the plants: 'Unless you eat me, you shall not have life in you.' If the grass and the herbs could speak, they would say to the animals: 'Unless you eat me, you shall not have life in you.' If the animals could speak, they would say to man: 'Unless you eat me, you shall not have life in you.' The whole evolutionary process becomes complete when the Word made flesh says to us: 'In truth, in very truth I tell you, unless you eat the flesh of the Son of Man and drink his blood, you can have no life in you' (John 6:54). Through the entire anabolic process, the lower is transformed into the higher; chemicals into plants; plants into animals; animals into man—and man into Christ.

"The other aspect of the Eucharist so often neglected is the catabolic—namely, death is the condition of life. The plants may say to the chemicals: 'You are inert, lifeless matter. Would you like to have life? Well, you cannot remain as you are; you must be changed; your nature must be surrendered; you must die to yourself. Then you can live in my kingdom.'

"If the animal could communicate, it would say to the plants: 'You have no power of locomotion, powerless as you are to move from the shadow to light.

Would you like to live a higher life, be reborn into a world where you can see and taste, smell, feel, touch? Well, you cannot do so as you are. You must be plucked up by the roots, ground like wheat between teeth before you can live in my kingdom.'

"Man, following the law, says to the animal: 'Would you like to be a thinking, living being, able to scan the stars with your wisdom? You cannot do it as you are. You must submit yourself to knife and fire, and then only can you live in me.' So Christ says to us: 'Unless you die to yourself, you cannot live in Me. No one who does not carry his cross and come with Me, can be a disciple of mine.' (Luke 14:27).

"These two biological and theological aspects of spiritual metabolism must be kept together to solve the mystery of the Eucharist which is both a sacrifice and a sacrament," he declared. Then he focused on Christ as the answer to the ecumenical

problem of the Eucharist: "I wonder if we have not too much stumbled at names—theological interpretations which form cataracts over our eyes. We have been more concerned in *what* is present than in *Who* is present. A loving husband and wife are not concerned with any Freudian or glandular explanation of their being two in one flesh. The important thing for us to do, who are surrounded with so many witnesses, as the Epistle to the Hebrews puts it, is to '. . . keep our eyes fixed on Jesus . . .' (Hebrews 12:2).

"Rilke tells us in one of his poems about a child sleeping in a room above his parents. The child awakes at night and feels solitary and alone, so he tosses in his bed, coughs, knocks a book on the floor to arouse the parents below. The good parent hears, of course, and brings the child a drink of water. The child is reassured. He is not alone, so he relaxes and falls to sleep.

"What is the floor that separated child and parent? It is our rational interpretation of the Eucharist, our cliches, our systematized, theological jargon, which close out the Eucharistic Lord as sacrifice and sacrament from us. By

dropping our books and pencils, we'll come to a greater understanding of this great sacrament of love. There are some things you have to experience; then you'll come to know. The great mysteries of God are understood in this way. If you're looking for faith in the presence of the Sacrament, go there, kneel down, be silent, let Him talk to you. He will convince you of his real presence. When some apostles first met our Lord, they asked Him, 'Where do you live' He said, 'Come and see.' That's what I say to you: 'Come and see!' "

Archbishop Sheen's talk was everything Mary Lenz, the Georgia grandmother, had hoped for. She was still murmuring, "Beautiful, just beautiful!" as she walked outside the Civic Center. When asked why she had decided to come such a long way to attend the congress, she replied, "For two reasons: I had never been to one before and after hearing my mother talk about one she went to as a girl, I wanted to go myself. But I also have a very dear friend who lives in a home in Philadelphia and has a bad heart condition. I wanted to visit her."

She said she had been quite sick the previous autumn at the time she decided to make the trip, and one of her daughters had said, "You'll never go, Momma."

"But I just felt I needed to be more spiritually motivated, to become more interested in the dear Lord Himself," Mrs. Lenz explained.

Word of the mystery illness that killed more than two dozen members of the American Legion attending a convention in Philadelphia hit the press before she left, and her husband, five children, and nine grandchildren tried to talk her out of going. "Everybody was calling," she said. "My daughter, a registered nurse, was calling madly, Peggy was calling Sissy, and Sissy was calling me, and the grandchildren were saying, 'Don't go, Grandmomma, don't go!' But I felt, well, if the dear Lord gives me my next breath, He can bring me home safely. If He wants

me to go, He wants me to go. I did call the Board of Health in Philadelphia, but they spoke in a Northern dialect and I spoke in a Southern dialect, so we had a little bit of trouble talking to each other. I said, 'I hear there's an epidemic in Philadelphia and people are being quarantined,' and she [the city official] nearly died laughing. She said, 'If there is, I haven't heard about it,' so I thought the press had blown it up."

Mary Lenz, who has a long-standing admiration for Archbishop Sheen, said, "I just thought his talk was the most wonderful thing, the most wonderful thing I ever heard. The woman who lived across the street from me was a Methodist, and we used to listen to him on television. She would come dashing across the street to say, 'He's on!' I had heard his cassettes at spiritual retreats and thought he was the greatest. I still think so, and he proved it today. And God bless him, his speech was short enough too."

Although it's still unusual to be a Roman Catholic in the heavily Protestant Deep South, "It's not as unusual as it used to be," she noted. The ecumenism down there is really great, especially between the Episcopalians and Catholics. Even the Baptists are coming around," she chuckled. "The big problem between the denominations has been that we were as standoffish of them as they were of us.

We were both leery of each other. There was definitely fault on both sides. But a change is taking place as we now emphasize what we agree on and de-emphasize the things that divide us.

"There's a real love of Jesus Christ, especially among the charismatics in our area. I'm not a charismatic myself, but I've been to some of their meetings, and I'd have a Presbyterian on one side and someone from another denomination on the other. When you hold hands and pray, you can feel the love of God forcing through. You become one, not just a group of individuals.

"We had a fight against pornography a few years ago, and the Roman Catholics led it as a citizens group, but my Methodist friend helped us. We had a Catholic priest, a Protestant minister and a rabbi. There's another fight going on now against obscene books, and the Methodists are leading that."

As she looked forward to the rest of the congress, Mrs. Lenz said she was hoping to enhance her spiritual life by concentrating on "the love of Christ in the Eucharist. I'm asking the most Sacred Heart of Jesus to touch everybody here. I've been praying that because so often I think we hear in this ear and it goes right out the other. The words of these [speakers] don't really motivate us enough."

Among the inspiring speeches on Christian unity that Mary Lenz and thousands of others heard that day was the address of Dr. Robert J. Marshall, the president of the Lutheran Church in America. He struck a response chord with his Catholic listeners at the Civic Center when he declared, "We must see the Lord Jesus Christ as the focus of our heritage, for *that* we have together. We do worship the same Lord. . . . God has turned our differences into channels of great value and purpose."

Dr. Marshall warned, though, that "love without truth is an abstraction, meaningless sentimentality, unstable in all its ways. God wants an honest pursuit together for unity of the church. We know we have only begun to walk together."

The optimistic, yet realistic words of this Lutheran leader were echoed in some private observations Leon Cardinal Suenens made to a team of *National Courier* interviewers. "When can all Christians commune together?" one editor asked.

"I hope that will come in the near future, but we still have to clarify some points," the cardinal replied. "And we must do that in all openness. We [the Roman Catholics] are very near to the Orthodox Church. There is just one question—the question of the papacy. But we have said to Catholics, 'You may have reasons on some occasions to take Communion with the Orthodox. For example, you may go to Russia as a tourist and find there is no other church but the Orthodox. In such circumstances,

Catholics are free to do it.' But they [the Orthodox] don't wish it. So you can't force it.

"On the other [Protestant] side, we must also proceed in all clarity. Although the question of the validity of the ministry is not solved, that is being worked out. But we cannot disassociate union from the Eucharist and the Church. The Church for us is Eucharistic reality. You can't say, 'I will take the Eucharist but I don't take the Church as a unity.' But progress is very, very strong, and I hope it will come. My dream is to see that before I go to heaven."

Many other participants in the Eucharistic Congress were dreaming the same dream on the night of the special Ecumenical Service. The highlight of the service was a footwashing ceremony, involving both Catholic and non-Catholic church leaders, as well as many lay people.

Jan Cardinal Willebrands, President of the Vatican Secretariat for Christian Unity, summarized the purpose of the observance in his homily when he noted that mankind was scattered around the earth after trying unsuccessfully to build the tower of Babel. "Sin alienated all human society from God and men from one another," he explained. "They tried to 'make a name' for themselves. It refers to rejection of dependence on God."

The reversal of this movement toward confusion and alienation, he said, was fulfilled on Pentecost, when obedient faith brought the nations together. But we have moved since that time into another period of disunity. "Considering the situation of our churches and communities, should we not with renewed intent pray for and aim at that 'renewal of

the Church which essentially consists in an increase of fidelity to her own calling'?" he asked, quoting the stated goals of the Second Vatican Council. "We must every day thank God for the ecumenical movement and never weaken or lose our hope in its final fruit, described eloquently by St. Paul and prayed for with utmost love by Jesus."

But the greatest goal of unity, sharing the Eucharist, which Vatican II extolled, still remains unfulfilled, Cardinal Willebrands admitted sadly. "Dear brothers and sisters in Christ, we can hardly take seriously enough the pain and grief that even on the occasion of this Eucharistic Congress we cannot celebrate all together the Lord's Supper. . . . This fact reveals to us the seriousness of the damage done to the seamless robe of Christ by our divisions. . . . This leads us to the Rite of Repentance in which we

will express together our sinfulness and our hunger for the common bread, which is the body of Christ in the communion of his Church. It prepares us also for the washing of the feet, the symbolic act of servanthood, performed by the Lord before He received as Host and Servant, his disciples for the Last Supper."

So it was with joy at ecumenical progress, but sadness at the lack of ulti-

mate fulfillment that scores of congress pilgrims took off their shoes and socks and participated in the washing of feet before the dais. William Cardinal Baum, the Archbishop of Washington, D.C., was there. So were the Most Rev. John M. Allin, presiding bishop of the Episcopal Church, U.S.A.; Dr. Robert J. Marshall, president of the Lutheran Church in America; and many others from a variety of denominations. The sight of these church leaders gathering

up their robes to wash and be washed deeply touched one nun, who identified herself only as Sister Josepha. With tears streaming down her cheeks and her eyes red from weeping, she said, "Ten years ago, you wouldn't have seen this. I think we're on our way. It seems only to be a matter of tradition. Somehow we forgot about our [common] heritage."

As the huge Civic Center auditorium resounded with the singing of "Amazing Grace" and other hymns from a variety of Christian traditions, one of the participants, Jane Hartsell, the wife of a Baptist pastor, said, "I think what impressed me most were the cardinals and the clergy coming down and washing feet. You know, about the greatest making themselves the least."

As he walked out in the informal recessional, another footwasher, Ray Peters, of St. Jerome's parish in Philadelphia, remarked, "It's great to see cardinals of the Catholic Church, Presbyterian ministers, Lutherans, together like this. It's fantastic! This is what the Mass is all

—

about. It's the reason we chose to attend this particular service." His two children and his mother-in-law had joined him in one of the small circles of footwashers at the front of the auditorium, and all seemed as enthusiastic as he was.

But as Cardinal Willebrands, Cardinal Suenens and others have cautioned, ecumenical progress should not obscure the fact that we are still falling short of the unity, the spiritual oneness that

Christ said should characterize His followers. The precise truth, the theological and ecclesiastical common denominator, has not yet been found to remove the pain of denominational division and bring us together at the same Holy Communion. Rather than becoming satisfied with only part of the truth and partial expressions of love, we must keep our sights set on the kind of unity that St. Paul endorsed in his "epistle of Christian unity," Ephesians 4:4-6: "There is but one body and one Spirit, just as there is but one hope given all of you by your call. There is one Lord, one faith, one baptism; one God and Father of all, Who is over all, and works through all, and is in all."

Hunger for Understanding

Let's sit down and talk it over." Too often these days this simple invitation is never offered or accepted—especially in family disputes. Instead, husbands and wives prefer to sulk or shout at each other; parents and children would rather squabble than come to agreement. Ineffective communication, which results in misunderstanding and severely damaged relationships, may be the biggest problem facing contemporary families.

Genuine, heartfelt communication is the only sure path to a real understanding of what makes another human being tick, and the best way to develop this ability to communicate is to learn at the feet of the best Communicator of all, the One who conveyed his love to us through his Son, Jesus Christ. Solomon was quite straightforward about the divine source of true understanding when he wrote in Proverbs 9:10 that ". . . knowledge of the Holy One is understanding."

When we put Jesus Christ first in our family life, the old battles between the sexes and the animosities between the old and the young, will begin to melt away. And the understanding, whose source is God, will be manifested through that ideal of love that St. Paul described in a classic passage in I Corinthians 13:4-7: "Love is patient; love is kind. Love is not jealous, it does not put on airs, it is not snobbish. Love is never rude, it is not self-seeking, it is not prone to anger; neither does it brood over injuries. Love does not rejoice in what is wrong but rejoices with the truth. There is no limit to love's forbearance, to its trust, its hope, its power to endure."

With this goal of divine love in mind, many of the husbands, wives, parents and children at the Philadelphia Eucharistic Congress attempted to open new channels of communication and understanding with one another.

FAMILY AFFAIRS

The regal presence of Princess Grace and Prince Rainier of Monaco was one of the highlights of the 41st International Eucharistic Congress. Every time the prince and his wife—the former Academy-Award-winning actress, Grace Kelly—appeared in public, the cameras would come out and the crowds would stare. Only Mother Teresa of Calcutta seemed to receive as much attention.

But the prince and princess were not there just to make a celebrity appearance. With their three children, Caroline, nineteen, Albert, seventeen, and Stephanie, eleven, they participated actively in the "Family Conferences" at the congress and enthusiastically endorsed the Christian faith as a firm foundation for homelife.

"I know for myself—marrying a man from a different country, different language, different culture and traditions— it would have been extremely difficult without the strong basic bond of our religion," the blonde princess declared. "It is essential to establish a fundamental discipline and respect within the family structure, and this is mainly the mother's job—not only to teach her children to respect the authority of the father as natural head of the family, but to respect

each other and to respect themselves."

She concluded that "the Christian family is of the utmost important and can be a strong and vital force in today's society, but we need help. We look hopefully to the Church for encouragement and guidance."

Prince Rainier, speaking "by personal experience as a man and a father," admitted he was "still learning each and every day" about what it means to be a parent. But he said that one important thing he has learned is that it's "essential to establish and maintain the dialogue between the parents and their child."

The prince also deplored the "terrible absence of Christ in the modern concept of life," and declared unequivocally that the "discipline in one's faith is the cement that keeps a family together, united in one common belief."

But Prince Rainier also warned that Christians must be steadfast and outspoken in supporting their faith at home. "There is no doubt in my mind that there is hope in the Christian family as long as we proclaim our want for it," he said. "But silent Christians are of little use and poor effect. . . . Yes, there is hope in the Christian family if we parents awaken and face the changes of the modern times that influence our family lives. We must adapt continually to the realities of our daily existence because to be a Christian is not to stay in one's corner, silent in prayer, trying to blindly obey God's commandments or going devotedly to church once a week and feeling cleansed. To be a real Christian is to go out, admit one's faith and fight for it. So I believe that a true Christian family is one united in the belief in Christ [and] strengthened by an unchangeable hope that by the love of God, He will give us each day our daily bread and that we will be delivered from all evil."

Prince Rainier and Princess Grace, who is a native of Philadelphia, were received warmly by the huge crowd at the Civic Center, and their observations and advice seemed to be a natural introduction to the Mass for Family Life that evening at Veterans Stadium.

Terence Cardinal Cooke, in delivering the homily to about twenty thousand people at the Mass, noted, "There are husbands and wives here who, inspired by the Holy Spirit, have reached out to each other in the Sacrament of Matrimony in a renewed common search to make their love grow deeper. They have helped each other and in many cases they have been encouraged by such rapidly expanding movements as Marriage Encounter. . . ."

At that point, wild cheering broke out in the audience. The reaction was evidence of how words and concepts from the altar can find resounding echoes of practical meaning in the lives of individual Christians. The Marriage Encounter movement is one of the most vital forces in contemporary Roman Catholicism and is a major vehicle that the Holy Spirit is using to foster deeper understanding between husbands and wives.

The tremendous impact of the Marriage Encounter movement is revealed most clearly in the lives of individual couples, like Jim and Joan Benjamin of Columbia, Maryland. Jim, who lets his dark hair grow over his collar and sports a flowing Zapata mustache, is a medical doctor, an internist. Joan, whose appealing freckles dance around sparkling gray eyes, is a former Toyota employee and has a penchant for feminism. They are both thirty-five and life-long Catholics; they have three wonderful kids (Jimmy, Debbie, and Christopher); and, by their own admission, their marriage was moving toward trouble three years ago.

"Joan and the kids were something I took for granted," Jim said. "I was in

research at the time and I thought I wanted to make a great scientific contribution."

"He wasn't listening to me, and I wasn't listening to him," Joan agreed. "I

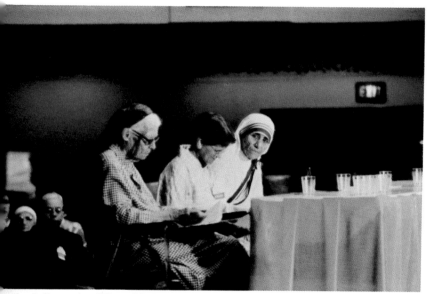

had discovered I couldn't have any more children, but I wanted more because I had come from a large family myself. I'm the oldest of eight children, and my parents loved me a lot, so I've always been able to love children. But because I had been told I couldn't give birth and because I was sure Jim didn't need me, I went out and got a job with Toyota and got into feminism."

Joan joined a consciousness-raising group and threw herself into the decision-making process of her local parish as vice-president of the parish board. "But all the while, there was this hunger in me for a child," she said. "The feminism was a substitute."

"I think for me, the experience in church was like that of many in our age group—there were rules and regulations, but I don't think my faith was a lived experience," Jim said. "I couldn't see the connection between going to Mass and living day by day."

So three years ago, eager to find some solution to their problems, the couple decided to give Marriage Encounter a try. Under the leadership of priests and other couples who had gone through the experience, they learned that they should rearrange their priorities. They had to begin to put each other first; and the more they grew together, the closer, in turn, that they would grow to God.

"The weekend was not a religious experience for me," Jim said. "It was very much a couple experience, though. Then we chose to go into a follow-up program and presented about sixteen weekends for other groups. That involved giving talks to other groups and gave us chances to look more into our relationship and strengthen it."

During these additional weekends, Joan noticed the religious experience becoming more important for Jim. "He began to grow in his relationship with God, but I still wasn't open to listening to him or to God either. But Jim kept moving me along, giving me hope. We tried to pray together, tried the charismatics. Part of our struggle was that he wanted to grow closer to the Lord and experience different [spiritual] situations, while I would say, 'I'm not going! If you want to read your books and talk to people, go ahead!' "

Joan's main problem, she said, was that she was still quite discontent and rather bitter about not being able to have another baby. "She had a physical scarring of both tubes, so nothing could get through," Jim explained with medical

precision. "One of the tubes had been opened two years before, but nothing happened, and the obstetrician told her it wasn't going to work. The operation is successful only ten to twenty percent of the time, and [then] pregnancy almost always happens within a few months of the operation."

"I was absolutely told by the doctors I wouldn't have a baby," Joan said. "My original physician told me to buy a dog."

Both Jim and Joan realize that it may seem unusual for a couple with three children already to be so eager to have more. "People think it's ridiculous," Joan admitted. "A lot of my friends have abortions—many of the women work and don't want to be tied down. But we came to the conclusion we have a lot to offer a family, and we really wanted to spend our energies in loving and caring for them."

But even as Joan's frustration deepened, so did Jim's faith. In fact, he received a strong impression, despite all negative medical predictions, that Joan *would* have a child. "I know it was somehow the Lord's strength coming through me," he explained. "I've always been able to tell Joan we were going to have a child, even though I didn't know how it would

happen. She's tried to pin me down, as though I were a fortune teller or something. She'd say, 'Is it going to be this way or that way?' and I'd say, 'I don't know.' And we'd have a lot of false hopes and discouragements."

One of those discouragements was an attempt at an adoption that failed. The Benjamins had even made plans to build a new home so that there would be enough room for the new child. Even though the adoption fell through, Jim, on faith, decided to go ahead with the home. "The baby wasn't coming, so I said 'Scratch the house,'" Joan recalled. "But Jim said,

'We're building it. We'll need that extra room because the baby will come.' I couldn't believe it, but he said, 'The room will be filled, I guarantee you.'"

Then a sequence of events began which Joan and Jim regard as "definitely" a miracle. Although they had never been

to Europe before, they decided to join a Marriage Encounter trip to Lourdes, France. In a great step of faith, Joan planned to bathe in the waters at the shrine there in the hope that she would be healed and be able to have a baby. She knew it would be important to have the prayers of Christian friends, so she wrote people around the country to ask their support. "It was difficult for me to ask," she admitted. "It wasn't that I didn't care that much, because I did. But it took me

love was really Christ's love, but I wouldn't listen."

"Every time we heard about some miracle, it seemed to grind the knife in more, twisted it," Jim remembered, grimacing at the thought of Joan's emotional anguish.

But despite all these misgivings, they traveled to Lourdes in the fall of 1975, and Joan went through the entire procedure at the shrine. She put all her prayer petitions in a basket at the cathedral, and then she prepared to bathe in the spring waters where Bernadette had reportedly encountered Mary, the mother of Christ. The baths are built into the side of a mountain, and consist of a series of rooms with curtained-off areas for bathing.

"I removed my clothes, and some women put a cloth around my shoulders and led me to a long, sunken bathtub, with stairs on either side," Joan explained. "The water was freezing cold, about two feet deep, and a woman on each side of me held my hands. I had to kiss a little statue, and then I went down into the water and was completely submerged, except for my head. When I

Joan also had a built-in prejudice against miraculous answers to prayer. "People had been telling us stories like this for three years in Marriage Encounter," she said. "I said, 'Fine for you,' and I'd get drowsy. I was sick of all those stories: 'Your mother is better, you're talking to your brother after twenty years.' These stories really turned me off. I hadn't had a personal experience of being loved myself because I couldn't accept Jim's loving me. I know now Jim's

months before I finally made the decision. Then I wrote to lots of people, called them up. I even wrote a letter to a local newspaper. It was hard, though, because I'm too proud for that kind of thing."

came out of the baths, I didn't dry myself before I dressed because they told me not to. And it was strange: I was actually dry when I walked out."

Joan and Jim returned home to Maryland, but nothing seemed to change. "The adoption hadn't worked out, and even though Jim was still growing in his relationship with the Lord, I wasn't as open to that," Joan recalled. "He asked me if I could praise the Lord for this cross I had to bear, and I said, 'No way! I can't thank Him for this hell!' But Jim kept asking me, gently. Then one night, through tears, I said, 'All right, Lord, I'll praise you for this, I'll praise you!'"

She became pregnant almost immediately.

"We're expecting on Thanksgiving," Joan said with a knowing smile. Under her nametag at the congress, she had added the words, "Plus Miracle." "We've seen a lot of people at the congress this weekend who have been praying for us, and tears come to their eyes when they see me."

"I'm convinced she has been physically healed," Jim declared. "We just

want to tell people how good the Lord is, how we've had the personal experience of being touched and healed by Him. I was convinced that Jesus loved Joan and that He was going to show her that love. Sometimes I felt like a Pollyanna when I kept saying He cares about you and everything will be okay. But that's part of what I'm praising Him for—being able to let me keep her hopes up.

"God wanted us to look at each other first. Joan was fighting the battle [about not being able to have a child] by herself before that first Marriage Encounter weekend three years ago. She didn't have any way to tell me, she couldn't share her problem. But then we entered a level of communication we hadn't achieved before, and I could feel her pain and separation and hurt. I experienced what it was like for her. As a result of the improvement in our relationship, we were able to depend more and more on the Lord, until finally we could praise Him through clenched teeth. And then the pregnancy. I think the Lord wanted us to go through this process."

Their new baby will be dedicated to God, "to show the Lord our gratitude," Jim says. At the christening, he himself plans to sing a song written by the Reverend Carey Landry, which has rather appropriate lyrics for the Benjamins: "Child of joy, child of pain, child of two becoming one."

The healing miracle that the Benjamins experienced in their marriage may be more dramatic than most. But the miracle of marriages transformed by the power of Christ is happening regularly in Marriage Encounter groups around the world. An estimated eighty-five hundred couples like Jim and Joan were at the Eucharistic Congress to testify to the benefits of the movement in their own lives. It's hard to argue with such success.

Although Joan Benjamin has changed a lot of her thinking about God and marriage during the past few months, she still considers herself a feminist and supports movements for women's rights within the Church. She found a great deal of support for her views at the congress, which reportedly was the first in history to include women on all its committees.

At the beginning of an all-day series of conferences on "Woman and the Eucharist," Sister Angelita Myerscough, said in the keynote address that there are "more than two billion women living today on earth. To Jesus in the Eucharist, each is known by name. For each of them Jesus offers to God unceasing thanks and praise. To each of them He offers that fullness of love and understanding, for which, like you and me, they all hunger. All of us need *understanding*. We need to understand ourselves, acceptingly, in our own unique personhood. We need to understand ourselves and one another in our essential interrelatedness, and in our

deep double restless yearning to realize our potential to make the world somehow better than we found it, and to find in death a meaning for life."

The world-renowned Dorothy Day, leader of the Catholic Worker Movement and co-publisher of the *Catholic Worker*, a monthly tabloid newspaper, asked that all present at the congress do penance in the liturgies on the anniversary of the bombing of Hiroshima. Humbly dressed in a mid-calf length skirt and wearing a paisley scarf on her head, she declared that all must do penance for our sins before we can approach God.

Mother Teresa, dressed just as humbly in her rough white cotton sari, followed Dorothy Day and greeted the inevitable ovation with head bowed and hands folded prayerfully. She concentrated at first on the virtues of Mary and then declared, "The beautiful compassion of a woman's heart—oh, to have compassion. You and I—do we use it? Am I like Mary?"

Then she told a "parable of the dusty lamp." It seems she was trying to help an old man in Australia when her sisters in the Missionaries of Charity were first establishing houses in that area. The old man had an unlighted lamp, covered with dust, so Mother Teresa asked, "Don't you light the lamp?"

"I have no one to light it for," he replied.

"If someone would come every night, would you light it?" she responded.

"Yes," he said, so the sisters began visiting him every night.

Mother Teresa forgot the incident,

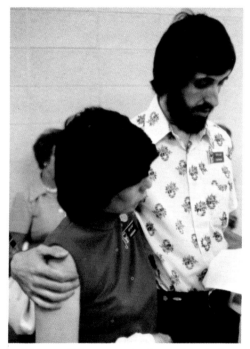

but years later she received a message from the old man saying, "Tell my friend the light she lit in my life is still burning."

There was not a dry eye in the audience when she finished the story.

As men and women try to understand themselves and their relationships with one another, it's inevitable that they will also have to confront the problems of younger friends and family members. To deal with this issue and recognize the importance of youth, the congress sponsored a Children's Mass and also a Youth Conference. One pilgrim at the congress who took to heart the need of young people for understanding by their elders was Sister Louista Etkroth, who teaches fifth grade at Christ the King school in Bismarck, North Dakota. While doing parish work one summer, she encountered a neglected high school girl who had developed many personal problems, primarily because her mother wasn't around home enough to give her proper guidance. "As we sat at a table in her home, she told me so many of her problems, really opened her heart up to me. She hadn't been to church in a long time; she was smoking and had developed other bad habits. So I asked if she'd like to pray with me, the Spirit really prayed through me as I asked that she find a way to solve her problems and return to the fold, to the Church.

"I learned when her birthday was and called her on that date. She was elated. We kept up contact, and finally, when I ran into her one day, she said, 'You know sister, I went to Mass Sunday.' I know the Holy Spirit was working in that relationship."

Sister Louista's story illustrates the central thread in all these accounts of the hunger for and discovery of understanding. The hungry person may be a senior citizen—and there was a Mass for senior citizens—or a divorced Christian or anyone else whose family ties have atrophied or been torn asunder. Whoever the needy individual, the only food that will satisfy his hunger permanently and completely must come from the healing power of God's Spirit, from the Living Bread, which is Jesus Himself. Or as Solomon expressed it in Proverbs 2:6, ". . . the Lord gives wisdom, from his mouth come knowledge and understanding."

"...my peace is
my gift to you..."

Hunger
for Peace

One of the greatest benefits of the Christian life is that inner calmness, that "peace which is beyond all understanding" (Phil. 4:7)—a peace which frees us from the anxieties and confusions of contemporary life. To experience such peace, it's necessary to develop a firm, unshakable faith, a completely obedient relationship with God. After this happens, our inner commitment will flow outward, and the peace we are enjoying in our deepest selves will touch those around us, envelop them, help them cast aside controversies and dissensions.

When Christ said, "Blest too the peacemakers; they shall be called sons of God" (Matthew 5:9), perhaps He had in mind this calm that flows from internal commitment to external action. We have already seen how guidance by God through the Holy Spirit can heal both rifts among different Christian denominations and problems in family relationships. But what about the multitude of interest groups that comprise the Roman Catholic Church itself? Can God's inner peace overcome the Church's inner threats of factionalism?

The Christian community has often faced the danger of disruption from special interest groups. St. Paul, for example, warned the church at Corinth, "Let there be no factions; rather, be united in mind and judgment. I have been informed, my brothers . . . that you are quarreling among yourselves" (I Corinthians 1:11). But Jesus gave us the key to resolving this difficulty when he told His disciples, " 'Peace' is my farewell to you, my peace is my gift to you; I do not give it to you as the world gives peace. Do not be distressed or fearful" (John 14:27).

Let's keep in mind the *full* meaning of Christ's gift to us—the freedom from inner anxiety as well as the power to be peacemakers—as we examine the exciting diversity of the Roman Catholic tradition at the 41st International Eucharistic Congress.

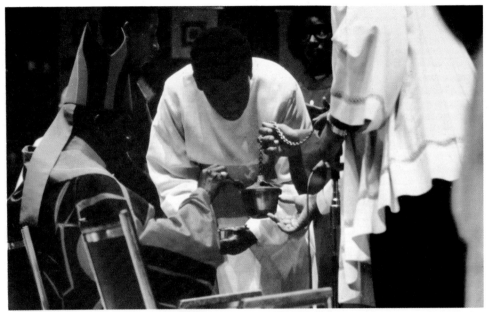

From the moment most visitors entered the exhibit hall at the Philadelphia Civic Center, they were struck by how many small "denominations" make up the Roman Catholic Church. Hundreds of religious organizations had put their activities on display in a colorful array of booths and literature racks.

The "Czech Catholics of Texas" had hung a Texas flag above their various religious artifacts.

Franciscan folk singers at the Christ House booth strummed guitars and sang, "You are the joy of Jesus in my life" to the crowds of visitors.

The Slovak Catholic School of Passaic, New Jersey, was there, and so was the Ukrainian Rite Order of St. Basil the Great.

Representatives of the Indian Participation Committee, U.S.A., decorated their assigned area with Western memorabilia and signs saying, "Custer Had It Coming" and "Indians Discovered America."

Author Louise D'Angelo and the Mary Heart Crusaders were displaying a crucifix that was reportedly more than three-hundred years old and had been

discovered on the site of the Church of the Nativity in Bethlehem. The author said she had been presented with the crucifix while giving a lecture in Florida.

At the back of the exhibit hall was a huge banner saying, "Win a Fantastic Trip to Rome for Two." Another sign over the booth read, "To qualify for the trip-for-two-to-Rome Sweepstakes, Act Now! Buy your first edition papal busts today."

There also were a number of non-Catholic organizations, such as Scripture Union and Logos, and various sellers of liturgical garments, choir robes and religious books. One of the hottest-selling volumes, as might be expected, was Malcolm Muggeridge's *Something Beautiful for God*, an account of Mother Teresa's work in Calcutta. One nun, a Sister Antoinette, said that the book was selling so fast she couldn't keep it in stock.

The effect on the casual visitor of being confronted by the incredible diversity of the Church was almost overwhelming. "How can all these groups possibly get along together?" was the most natural question. And the most

honest answer is, "Sometimes, they don't."

Even at the congress, there were a few rumblings of unrest. Some Ukrainian Catholics were upset because Joseph Cardinal Slipyj, who had been confined in Soviet prison camps and then released, was not present in Philadelphia. A congress spokesman explained that any appearance or speech by the cardinal might endanger Roman Catholics in the Ukraine, which is controlled by the U.S.S.R. But a number of Ukrainians carried signs at the congress events charging, "The Vatican Discriminates Against the Ukrainian Catholic Church!" There was also a brief protest with bullhorns that interrupted one of the sessions in the Civic Center.

Nor were the Ukrainians the only dissatisfied group. There was also a peaceful demonstration at the Military Mass celebrated in the Cathedral of Saints Peter and Paul. A peace organization was protesting because the event was being held on the anniversary of the atomic bombing of Hiroshima. The demonstrators felt the day should be one of mourning, rather than a celebration of the Eucharist by the military.

Despite these few signs of discontent, the face that the congress turned to the outside world was, for the most part, one of amazing harmony for a Church with such a myriad of life styles and divergent interests. There was some disagreement between black Catholics and congress officials over the extent to which the traditional liturgy should be changed for a Black Heritage Mass. But most of the difficulties were soon ironed out, and the consensus of those who attended was that this celebration of "The Gift of Negritude" was one of the high points of the congress.

As the African drums near the altar rolled, song leader Avon Gillespie, attired in a bright red robe, shouted, "If you don't believe it, you can't sing it!"

The crowd at the Spectrum responded with an exuberant rendition of "Hallelujah, hallelujah, hallelujah, amen; Thank the Lord for the Holy Spirit, who revives my soul again!"

There was a distinctive soul-beat to all the music, and many of the priests and bishops who marched in during the processional could be seen skipping a beat, or clapping to the music. One of the most exhilarating of the songs was the opening

hymn, "Spirit of Life," a toe-tapper with a chorus that went like this: "Spirit of life, spirit of love, soul of the living, heart of the loving. Make us into a soul people, new born again!"

Chief soloist Arthur Patterson, a tall, lean man with a range of sounds and voice techniques that frequently brought admirers in the audience to their feet, helped build the musical excitement as he answered each rendition of the "Spirit of Life" chorus with a new interpretation of some stanzas of the song.

Father Clarence Rivers of Cincinnati directed the Mass and wrote much of the music. He was a constant presence on the podium, encouraging the audience and the participants to throw themselves

wholeheartedly into this very special celebration of the Eucharist.

Several of the black priests and bishops wore special vestments designed in the black liberation colors of red, green and black, and the chief celebrant was

Maurice Michael Cardinal Otunga, Archbishop of Nairobi. The homily by Bishop Eugene Marino, Auxiliary Bishop of Washington, D.C., seemed to crystallize in words the strong, exuberant emotions that had gripped the audience.

"It is at this special moment in history that black peoples, who were previously oppressed within Mother Africa or scattered and oppressed in exile, have

now begun to reestablish their nation-hood, to reestablish their contacts with one another . . . to rediscover that they share in common a manifestation of the Spirit that we call soul or Negritude," he said. "It is at this special moment in history when many people are coming to realize that the culture of black peoples is a sacrament of the Spirit; and that the soulfulness, the spirit, the spiritual dynamism always so evident in happenings among black peoples, is precisely the element that is so frequently lacking elsewhere, both within and without the Church."

Referring to a speech by Representative Barbara Jordan and a prayer by Martin Luther King, Sr., at the recent Democratic National Convention, Bishop Marino said, "There were moments of inspiration, moments when the breath of the Spirit softened hearts. It is these moments that typify what the gift of Negritude, the gift of soul could mean to the Church. It is such soul-fulfilling inspiration that black members of the Body of Christ can bring with them for the uplifting of all Christ's members as they gather around the table of the Lord for the breaking of bread. It is such dew of the Spirit that can bring life to dry bones."

The spirit of enthusiasm and good will permeated all who partook of Holy Communion at the end of the service. Gospel choruses swept through the congregants, under the leadership of Avon Gillespie: "This little light of mine, I'm going to let it shine . . . I will trust in the Lord until I die . . . Plenty good room, plenty good room, plenty good room in my Father's Kingdom. . . ."

The tears that flow when the Spirit is moving were on the cheeks of many, both white and black, as the bishops, priests and cardinals filed out, clapping and waving, during the recessional. The Black Liturgy was one of the best examples at the congress of how diversity can bring a more exciting kind of unity to the Church; how out of many, One can emerge to tie us all together.

On other occasions, Philadelphia resounded with a variety of special ethnic services and celebrations. One of the most moving of these was the Na-

tive American Liturgy, which took place under a multi-peaked white tent on Independence Mall, a tent which reminded at least one observer of a giant butterfly's wings. Nearly five thousand people attended this ceremony, in which twenty-one different American Indian tribes participated. The opening procession dazzled the onlookers with its endless array of furs, feathers, beads, braided long hair, embroidery, buffalo headresses and bandanas.

Mother Teresa of Calcutta was there. So was Cardinal Knox, the Papal Legate. But the center of attraction was the Indians, with the dignity and pride of their history etched on their faces. Their cultural traditions merged with Christian truth as one of the Indian leaders offered a prayer with a peace pipe. He turned in each of the four directions and lifted the pipe as he prayed; then he gave the pipe to Cardinal Knox as a gift for the pope.

During the offertory procession, twenty-one Indians, each representing the tribes present, laid gifts—pottery, chalices, jewelry, a drum head—on an

Indian rug before the altar. Then came the most impressive part of the liturgy—the native American dances. Two men carrying gourd rattles and wearing huge buffalo headdresses, danced the San Juan

Pueblo Buffalo Dance. Two women also joined them in this expression of the importance of the buffalo to their forefathers for food, clothing and shelter.

Even more colorful headdresses were used in the Laguna Pueblo Eagle Dance. As five men simultaneously danced the same steps, eagle feathers trailed down their arms and wafted about in their movement. Sister Gloria Davis, who organized the entire service, explained that this dance suggests to her the gifts of the Holy Spirit. When the audience applauded enthusiastically after the Eagle Dance, though, she rushed to the microphone and cautioned, "All our dances are prayers, not performances.

Please do not clap!" But the appreciative congregation forgot her words and clapped anyhow after the next presentation.

This native American liturgy was not just a colorful show, however, for many of the American Indians present there and at other events of the congress were quick to show that their faith in Christ runs far deeper than mere cultural tradition. One of these was Ella Bordeaux, a Rosebud Sioux Indian from

White River, South Dakota, who wore a beaded headband during the congress and a beaded sign proclaiming, "Praise the Lord."

She said that her faith deepened a few years ago when she discovered the power of the Holy Spirit in her life. "I wanted a book with prayers to different

saints," she explained. "There was a litany to the Holy Ghost in the book, and I thought to myself, 'That's the first prayer I've ever seen to the Holy Ghost.' I got to wondering whether anybody ever prays to Him. So I started saying that litany— out of pity, I guess—because I didn't think anybody ever prayed to the Holy Ghost."

She now belongs to a prayer group at the St. Ignatius Mission at White River, and has been trying to raise money for her little parish, which has about thirty families. She even arranged to take some extra plastic spoons at the exhibit hall cafeteria back to her parish. "[We'll] recycle them," she said.

Like many other pilgrims at the congress, Ella was able to attend the event because of an answer to prayer. One of her companions, Sister Genevieve Cuny—who is an Oglala Sioux Indian herself and works on the Rosebud Sioux Reservation in South Dakota—said she was determined to go to the congress and also bring some of her friends. Sister Genevieve said she trusted in the Lord and then approached a priest, who gave her seven names of people who might provide the money. She wrote to these benefactors, and one responded with enough funds for six people to attend.

"God does take care of us if we have complete trust in Him," Sister Genevieve said. "God will provide for His little ones. We are God's little ones, and He will take care of us."

The words of this Sioux nun might well be applied to the binding force—the Holy Spirit—that tied together all the diverse traditions at the congress. And for the various ethnic groups, perhaps the best symbol of the unifying power of the Spirit was the Cursillo Movement, which originated in Spain during the 1940s and now claims a half million "Cursillistas," or participants in the United States, about twenty-five percent of whom are Spanish-speaking.

Cursillo, or "a short course in Christianity," begins with a long weekend, Thursday night through Sunday evening. There are fifteen talks on such topics as piety, ideals, sacraments, and the Christian community, but the main purpose is to help those present develop a personal relationship with Jesus Christ. An "ultreya," or visible gathering of the Cursillistas, was sponsored with the approval of the congress at Robin Hood Dell (West), the huge outdoor theater in Philadelphia. Among those present was Mrs. Mary

Bernardo, of Glassboro, New Jersey, who was one of the first three women from her area to make a Cursillo back in 1965.

"For me, it was a rebirth of my life," she declared. "When I made Cursillo, we didn't know anything about it. I was happy before, I always knew Christ was with all of us. But after that weekend, I knew He was with me *personally*."

She explained that Jesus had now become "my lover, my brother, my spiritual guide. He's my comforter, and also supplies me with all my needs. I just let Him give to me what He thinks I need. One of the things He did for me was let my husband make his Cursillo, too. I envy the young couples who have made a Cursillo or Marriage Encounter for the opportunity they have to raise their family. They don't have fear in raising a family. With Cursillo or Marriage Encounter, you learn not to worry so much, and to have your trust in God. And when you show children love, they will give it back to you."

The benefits of Cursillo are not limited to the young, though, according to the forty-nine-year-old Mrs. Bernardo. "A lot of older people think they don't need it, but it would give them a new lease on life, more peace and contentment. They can be more satisfied with the fact that they did raise their family and can now share together with one another. Most people, when they get older, don't know what to do. They just sit there." She noted that her mother, who is sixty-nine, made her Cursillo about four years ago.

Mrs. Bernardo also said she's no longer afraid to walk in ghetto sections after having experienced a Cursillo. "In a ghetto area, all I have to holler is 'De Colores,' and I'll be saved," she said. "De Colores," or "of the colors," is the slogan of the movement and may be taken to mean all the colors of God's love. For Mrs. Bernardo, "De Colores" symbolizes the connection between our present-day life and the life in Christ we can attain.

So as the various ethnic and historical traditions at the Philadelphia con-

gress moved toward the final event, the "Statio Orbis," which would mark the conclusion of the eight-day celebration, they moved as one. The peace that ruled the hearts of individuals because of their personal relationships with Jesus, expanded outward to tie people and entire cultures to one another in love. For a time, hundreds of thousands of pilgrims from every corner of the earth seemed to be giving a resounding "Yes!" to the urging of St. Paul in Colossians 3:15: "Christ's peace must reign in your hearts, since as members of the one body you have been called to that peace."

"I myself
am the living bread
come down
from heaven."

Hunger for Jesus

In teaching at the synagogue in Capernaum, Jesus made some rather straightforward claims about Himself. He said He was "the bread of life," or the "living bread," sent down from heaven by God the Father.

Many of those in his audience, including a number of disciples, seemed not to understand what He was saying. More likely, they didn't want to understand.

Why did these people object so strenuously to this offer of eternal life? Probably because Jesus required the most difficult thing for any human being to give—complete obedience and commitment to an outside authority. We have a deep inner need to exercise control over our own lives, to "play god" in the small sphere of our daily existence. Of course, we can never really determine our own destinies: Something always happens to make our carefully laid plans go awry. When this happens, we may begin to get a truer perspective on our largely impotent and finite human condition.

When we finally make that decision to acknowledge Jesus as Lord and to follow Him wherever He leads us, He will guide us to his table, where each of us must say, "Yes, I *do* need something outside myself. I will accept this living bread, this mystery that my mind can't fully understand." The Eucharist thus becomes the focal point for our obedience to God or "the center and crown of Christian life," according to *The Teaching of Christ: A Catholic Catechism for Adults* (Our Sunday Visitor Inc., Huntington, Ind., 1976; p. 420). This catechism continues: "For in the Eucharist Christ gives Himself to us, and we lay hold of Him. The Eucharist is not merely a symbol and ceremony; it is the sacrament in which, most of all, the saving works of Jesus and the gifts of God are made accessible to men."

These or similar thoughts were emerging in the minds of many pilgrims as the final day dawned on the 41st International Eucharistic Congress in Philadelphia.

THE LIVING BREAD

It had the makings of a terrible day. The heavens had unleashed all their fury to pour torrents of rain down on Philadelphia on Sunday morning. The Statio Orbis—or "assembly of the world" which has been the unique closing ceremony for every international congress since that first one in Lille, France, in 1881—seemed in danger of being washed out. The prospect that bad weather might dampen the enthusiasm of pilgrims from around the globe seemed especially disappointing since the weather had been so perfect throughout the rest of the week.

But the Providence which had watched over the activities and inspired personal spiritual experiences during the first days of the congress had sufficient blessings in store to cover the final Eucharistic celebration at John F. Kennedy Stadium. The rain eased, then ceased entirely, and a cool breeze swept through the huge stadium as more than one hundred thousand worshipers took their seats under a beautiful, billowing cover of clouds.

Considerable work had been invested in preparing an appropriate setting for this massive, diversified gathering of God's people. A gold altar platform rose about fifty feet at one end of the stadium and was set like some exotic jewel against a broad, blue and gold, beveled base that housed a large choir and supported a towering white cross. Thousands of chairs covered the playing field, and countless, colorfully-clad representatives of various ethnic groups and organizations sat in specially-designated sections of the bleachers.

The procession began as the choir sang "Crown Him With Many Crowns" over several huge loudspeakers that pro-

duced a stereophonic effect for the voices. The marchers in the procession included representatives of fifty states and fifty nations, with each group of authentically-costumed marchers carrying a distinctive state or national flag. One of the main highlights at the beginning of the service was the arrival of President Gerald Ford, who delivered a ten-minute address from a platform next to the altar.

"On this occasion we celebrate the Church's contribution to building a more peaceful world," the President told the crowd. "We salute you for giving depth and direction to the world community in every age. For millions of men and women, the Church has been the hospital for the soul, the school for the mind, and the safe depository for moral ideals."

The most enthusiastic response to President Ford's speech came when he took what his listeners interpreted as an anti-abortion position. "We are rightly concerned today about the rising tide of secularism across the world. I share your deep [apprehension] about the increased irreverence for life," he said, and was greeted by sustained applause and cheering from the audience.

James Cardinal Knox, the Papal Legate who acted as celebrant, opened the religious part of the service with a greeting. Then priests, dressed in the congress's distinctive yellow stoles and white chasubles with wheat symbols, moved through the crowd sprinkling holy water and offering blessings to the congregants.

Then came the moment which tied the entire week together, the time when Pope Paul VI spoke in a highly personal way via satellite to every individual in this great "assembly of the world."

146

"It is the Bishop of Rome who speaks to you, the successor of the Apostle Peter, the Pope of the Catholic Church, the Vicar of Christ on earth," he said. "He speaks to greet you, to assure you of his prayers, to have you hear in his voice the echo of Christ's word, and thus, to some extent, to open up to you the deep meaning of the mystery that you are celebrating.

"We ask you to be silent, to be silent now and to try to listen within yourselves to an inner proclamation:

"The Lord is saying: 'Be assured, I am with you' (Matthew 28:20). I am here, He is saying, because this is my body! This is the cup of my blood!

"The mystery of his presence is thus enacted and celebrated, the mystery of his sacramental, but real and living pre-

sence. Jesus, the teacher of humanity, is here; He is calling for you (John 11:28).

"Yes, He is calling you, each one by name! The mystery of the Eucharist is, above all, a personal mystery: personal, because of his divine presence—the presence of Christ, the Word of God made man; personal, because the Eucharist is meant for each of us. For this reason, Christ has become living bread, and is multiplied in the sacrament, in order to be accessible to every human being who receives Him worthily, and who opens to Him the door of faith and love.

"The Eucharist is a mystery of life! Christ says, 'He who eats this bread shall live!' (John 6:51). The Eucharist is a mystery of suffering, yes, and a mystery of death! A mystery of redemptive passion;

a mystery of sacrifice, consummated by Christ for our salvation. It is the mystery of the cross, reflected and commemorated in the sacrament which makes us share in the Lord's immolation, in order to associate us in his resurrection. Today, in time, the Eucharist is the food for our earthly pilgrimage; tomorrow, in the life to come, it will be our everlasting happiness.

"The Eucharist, is, therefore, a mystery of love. It makes all of us who eat the same bread into a single body (I Corinthians 10:17), living by means of one Spirit. It makes us one family: brothers and sisters united in solidarity with one another (Ephesians 4:16), and all of us dedicated to giving witness, in mutual love, to the fact that we really are followers of Christ (John 13:35).

"May it always be this way, beloved brethren, and sons and daughters!

"With our apostolic blessing, in the name of the Father, and of the Son, and of the Holy Spirit. Amen!"

The pope's words seemed to express the feelings of many of the pilgrims at JFK Stadium, from the most prominent cardinals to the most obscure parishioner. Many of them *had* experienced the

personal presence of Christ at the week-long Eucharistic celebrations, and Pope Paul's message provided them with the Church's affirmation of their inner spiritual discoveries.

The Statio Orbis proceeded with

hymns and the "General Intercessions" in a variety of languages—including English, French, Vietnamese, Italian, and Polish. Then, to the accompaniment of hand-bells, the words of the congress hymn, "Gift of Finest Wheat," moved softly and gently over the loudspeakers and into the audience: "You satisfy the

hungry heart with gift of finest wheat; come give to us, O saving Lord, the bread of life to eat. . . ."

Priests, bearing the consecrated hosts, spread out through the audience, and soon other Holy Communion songs rose from the stadium. Thousands raised their hands heavenward during the chorus, "And I will raise Him up, and I will raise Him up, and I will raise Him up on the last day!" Each individual praised God in his own way during this special moment. As one man stretched his arms to the sky, his sports coat slipped down to reveal a military tattoo on one wrist; a string of rosary beads, with a crucifix attached, dangled from between two of his fingers. Not far away, a stylishly-attired young woman with a perfectly shaped coiffure raised her hands just above her head, palms upward, as though in supplication to the Lord. Several rows in front of her, an elderly nun bowed her head reverently in her hands. Each approached God in a different posture; yet they were one in the body of Christ.

Then for the first time during the entire service, just as the priests were returning from serving Holy Communion, a light shower fell on the crowd. It was almost as though God Himself had decided to give his final blessing on the Statio Orbis. A forest of multi-colored umbrellas arose around the stadium, and

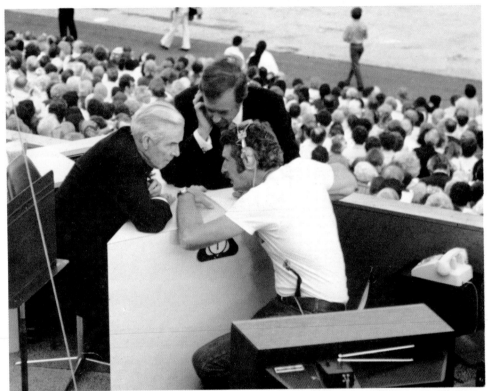

there were mostly smiles on the faces underneath. At the end of the Mass, John Cardinal Krol summed up the feelings of all when he declared, "We thank the Lord for holding the umbrella over our heads, and if He wants to soak us now, I'm willing."

But He didn't want to soak them. The shower soon stopped, and the thousands of pilgrims from the far reaches of the earth streamed out with inspiration in their hearts and thanksgiving on their lips.

One of those who had felt tremendous inspiration during the entire week to give thanks for Jesus, the Living Bread

was a young man who had come from Canada to attend the congress. His heart was farther away still, in his native Czechoslovakia. He gave his name as "Marian Krizan," but he explained quickly that this was a pseudonym. His real name, as well as his profession, would have to remain a secret, he explained, because his mother and father still lived in Czechoslovakia. Their safety would be jeopardized if the Communist authorities there learned their son was talking to the American press.

"My parents are both Christians, Roman Catholics, and my mother is quite devoted," he explained. "They're both still alive, God bless them. I attended my first religious courses in my country, but if you want to send your children, you must give your name, address, and employer. You risk loss of your job or being stopped in advancement of your profession. It's very hard—requires heroism for those parents who send their children to these courses. They have to have deep faith because you can't be a hero of Christ unless you have deep faith."

As he finished his religious studies, Marian discovered he had "a gift of faith, but the troubles of adolescence were always fighting against my convictions. I believe it was Christ's grace, given to me through his mother, who is our spiritual mother, and through my mother, that saved me from becoming misled and getting too far from Him. Whenever I started to sin, God always blocked my way so that the sin was never culminated. This was the crossroad of my young life, but I found I couldn't escape from God."

After passing through the trials and temptations of adolescence, Marian met his next big challenge when he began to grapple with whether or not to try to leave his country. "There was a great fight in my heart about whether I did good or evil," he said. "If I left my own country when it was in trouble, I wondered whether I might not be guilty of a lack of spirit of fraternity and brotherhood with my compatriots. But I overcame these feelings and got out just after the Russian invasion when I was twenty-five years old."

The young refugee eventually immigrated to Canada, and his faith in Christ continued to grow. When presented with the opportunity to travel to

Philadelphia for the congress, he decided to go because "I love Christ in the Eucharist. I wanted to worship Christ during one entire week on my holidays, which would be real 'holy days' for me. Imagine, the idea that many people from this city, the other states and other parts of the world would come together to think on this beautiful gift that Christ has given us. I would like to see all the people of this globe find this way, which leads to life.

Unfortunately, a lot of our human brothers are starving because of a lack of this bread of life, a lack of faith.

"At this congress, I am growing closer to Christ, and He will give me more grace to collaborate with Him. For me, the great key for this growth is the Eucharist, the physical contact with

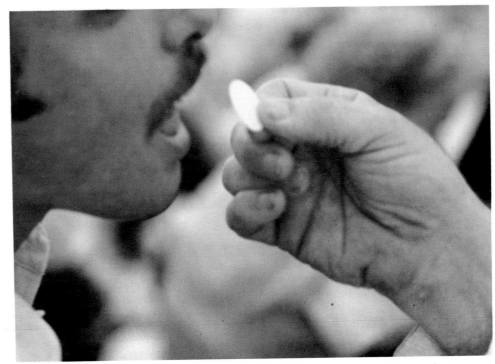

Christ. He is present, *really* present, and the bread is really changed into his body at the moment of consecration. My trip to Philadelphia reflects my desire to live more consistently with what I believe.

Christ becomes so real to me that sometimes it seems that only a very thin curtain separates me from Him."

An important factor enabling Jesus, the Living Bread, to permeate Marian's life is his daily devotions. "The formula for my spiritual life each day begins in the morning with a prayer and a few verses from the Bible. I ask the Holy Spirit to lead me, and then I ponder on the bread, the few verses. The words must go through the intellect and the reason to the heart," he said, closing his eyes and gesturing from his eyes down to his chest. "Usually, I close my eyes to avoid being distracted by the things before me, even if they are only the pictures on my wall. Then, I let the words of Scripture rest in my mind.

"Sometimes, it's easy for me to grasp food from the words. Other times, because of human weakness, the time is not so profitable, not so efficient. But I try to let the Holy Spirit ask my conscience, 'Marian, how well have you been living by the Bible passage you just read?' All this takes me about fifteen minutes, and then at the end I concentrate on decision making: 'What will I do today, very concretely and realistically, with my friends and at my work, to live by the words I have read?' When I make my decision, arrive at my conclusions, I write down some words on a piece of paper and put it in my pocket to remind me of my meditation. I believe God, through the Holy Spirit, gives me that message, and I ask Him to give me the strength to follow it."

While at the congress, Marian continued to follow his meditation procedure by using a small booklet which was written by a French nun several hundred years ago. He meditated on the passages and let the Holy Spirit use it like Scripture in his heart. And as he moved from one liturgy, one speech, one activity to another, a message gradually took shape in his mind, a message that he initially thought was directed only to him personally but which we might take as a prophetic utterance for all the pilgrims in Philadelphia and as a fitting benediction for the Statio Orbis itself:

"What has become imperative in my heart and what Christ was telling me is this: 'Marian, don't lose yourself in the happenings, the little exhibitions, the convention hall activities. Concentrate on Me. Concentrate on Me. Concentrate on what is the center of this congress, and it's Me—Me present among you, the saved people of this busy twentieth century. You live in concrete and steel, and you are so busy, going out and coming back. But concentrate on Me and grasp whatever you can from Me and this very special matter of my presence among you. Concentrate on what I saved on a

cross over there in Jerusalem one Good Friday and on that gift the night before on Holy Thursday. Concentrate on what I gave you that evening there, before I went to the Garden of Gethsemane and took all your sins—past, present and fu-

ture. I'm so happy you are celebrating here in Philadelphia this gift that I gave you."

May that gift, the Eucharist, become as important to us as it was at that moment to one Czechoslovakian refugee. And may Jesus, the Living Bread, someday be glorified at a Statio Orbis of all mankind.

'So they set out and went from village to village, spreading the good news everywhere...'

The 41st International Eucharistic Congress was a time for spiritual nourishment, for renewing faith and discovering new dimensions in the relationship between God and man. For many, it was a period of revaluation, of asking, "Am I going in the direction You want me to go, Lord? Am I doing the things that You want me to do?"

Most of the one million pilgrims who passed through Philadelphia had some hunger when they arrived, and few who had genuinely searched for God's answers, left unsatisfied. Those who came as tourists may have received some enjoyment from the Bicentennial sights in the historic city; but the true pilgrims left with much more. They streamed out of town after the Statio Orbis with their hungry hearts, their discontented or confused lives, filled by the ultimate source of man's hope, that Living Bread, Jesus Himself.

But the sumptuous spiritual banquet on which these serious Christians dined—and on which all of us can dine through a personal relationship with Christ—did not end at the table. All spiritual food, all strengthening of faith, empowers us to act more vigorously, forcefully and decisively for the Lord in our daily lives. Remember that St. James said, ". . . Faith without works is as dead as a body without breath" (James 2:26)—or without the Bread of Life, he might as easily have added. In other words, a genuine faith experience with Christ, a total commitment to Him, *has* to lead us to comfort the sick and feed the hungry, as Mother Teresa of Calcutta has so often stressed. Otherwise, our faith is not faith at all, but a hollow shell, a nominal, lip-service religion.

The final thought in our minds, as we leave the congress, should be this: After we've gathered together in Jesus' name and strengthened our relationship with Him, we must move out into the world and act on our convictions. Jesus' disciples in Luke 9:1-6 present a good example of what is expected of us. First of all, they submitted to his authority and accepted the power He delegated to them to overcome demons and cure diseases. Then, they listened to his instructions—special, rather strict instructions for that particular mission. Finally, when "He sent them forth to proclaim the reign of God and heal the afflicted," they were successful. Luke tells us that "they set out and went from village to village, spreading the good news everywhere and curing diseases."

Many pilgrims in Philadelphia also concentrated on becoming more obedient to Christ and on listening to his guidance for their lives. But as the last sounds of the Communion hymns at the Statio Orbis died away, the time arrived for them to act, just as Jesus' disciples had done. They returned to their jobs as nurses, homemakers, teachers and businessmen with the resolute intention of transforming their daily occupations into ministries, channels of action for God's work on earth.

This movement from "spiritual rest," as Dom Helder Camara might put it, to effective action is natural and essential for the Spirit-filled, wholly-committed Christian. It's unthinkable for God's vineyard not to bear the fruit of the Spirit, or for the salt of the earth to be kept bottled up in a saltshaker. We consume the Living Bread not to grow fat and lazy, but to gain spiritual power and energy so that God can use us to help bring others to Himself. Is it possible to imagine Mother Teresa dwelling only on her own spiritual development and not on helping the unfortunate who are "Jesus in the distressing disguise of the poor"?

The message of the congress is that every Christian—whether a Philadelphia pilgrim or a believer who has never seen the United States—must first experience Jesus in the Eucharist and then experience Him in the world. Christ requires our obedience in both endeavors; He has instructed us clearly as both worshipers and workers.

So let us be attentive to the invitation Christ has given us to dine on the Living Bread. We should be sure to get the directions to his Father's House right and to be on time for the dinner party. Above all, let us be careful not to offer weak excuses as to why we cannot attend. Remember Jesus' parable of the dinner guests, who concocted all sorts of incredible reasons for not going to a banquet (Luke 14:15-24). The ones who turned down their invitations didn't get a second chance, for the master of the house decided, "not one of those invited shall taste a morsel of my dinner.' "

So it is with the Eucharistic banquet Christ offers us. The invitations have been sent out, and we are on the guest list. Those who have not yet responded to the Host must accept quickly, lest they miss the only meal which can provide eternal life. And then let us continually respond to Jesus, the Living Bread, with the enthusiasm of St. Thomas Aquinas, who prayed . . .

'. . . I implore you to lead me to
that ineffable banquet where together
with your Son, the Holy Spirit,
and all the saints you are the
true light, complete contentment,
supernal joy, complete delight, and
perfect happiness.'

157

APPENDIXES

Staff Organization of the 41st International Eucharistic Congress August 1-August 8, 1976, Philadelphia, Pennsylvania

Chairman of the Board of Governors / His Eminence John Cardinal Krol, Archbishop of Philadelphia
Executive Vice Chairman / The Most Rev. Martin N. Lohmuller, Auxiliary Bishop of Philadelphia
Executive Secretary / Rev. Monsignor Walter J. Conway
Associate Executive Secretary / Robert H. Palestini
Assistant Executive Secretary / Raymond J. O'Brien

Coordinators

Spiritual Renewal & Preparation / Rev. W. Ronald Jameson
   Assistant / Sister Kathleenjoy Cooper
Program / David W. Schafer
Liturgy / Rev. Monsignor Charles J. McManus
   Associate Coordinator / Sister Barbara Pengitore
Sites / Rev. Monsignor H. Glenn Bennett
   Assistant / Miss Barbara Rosati
Performing Arts / Rev. Louis A. D'Addezio
Transportation / William A. Costello
   Assistant / William Marron
Housing & Tickets / Spencer E. Gautney
   Assistant / Bartholomew E. Lorenzo
Liturgical Art / Sister Paul Marie
Special Interest Groups / Thomas W. Ball
Volunteer Personnel / Sister Marguerite Schneider
   Assistant / Mrs. Dorothy K. McFadden

Directors & Managers

Office Manager / Miss Jane M. Keenan
Director of Music / Dr. Peter La Manna
Director of National Choir & Orchestra / Sister Walter M. Cadogan
Manager of Exhibits / Sister Catherine FitzPatrick
   Assistant / James P. McCarvill, II

Note:
In our attempt to balance the eight Hunger chapters of this book, the
National Courier staff has taken the liberty of using various stories, anecdotes,
homilies, interviews, and speeches from pilgrims that coincide with chapter themes
but do not always coincide with the days of the week in which the themes were
presented at the Congress. Our readers, however, might be interested to
know that the Hunger themes at the Congress were presented this way: *The
Eucharist and the Hunger for God*, Sunday, August 1, 1976; *the Eucharist and
the Hunger for Bread*, Monday, August 2, 1976; *the Eucharist and the Hunger
for Freedom and Justice*, Tuesday, August 3, 1976; *the Eucharist and the
Hunger for the Spirit*, Wednesday, August 4, 1976; *the Eucharist and the
Hunger for Truth*, Thursday, August 5, 1976; *the Eucharist and the Hunger for
Understanding*, Friday, August 6, 1976; *the Eucharist and the Hunger for
Peace*, Saturday, August 7, 1976; and *the Eucharist and the Hunger for Jesus,
the Bread of Life*, Sunday, August 8, 1976.

PHOTOGRAPHY CREDITS

Photographers for this book were Stephen B. Allen, Craig Callan, Thurman Mason, John Murello, William Proctor, and Richard Taylor.

Credits from left to right are separated by semicolons, from top to bottom by dashes.

Cover design: John Murello

Prologue
9-Chicago Tribune; 10 All-Callan; 11-Chicago Tribune; 12-Chicago Tribune; 13-Taylor, Murello; 14-Religious News Service.

Hunger for God
15-Callan; 17-Murello; 18-Mason; 19-Callan, Taylor; 20-Callan; 21-Callan; 22-Taylor; 23-Callan; 24-Callan; 25-Taylor; 26-Callan; 27-Callan; 28-Taylor; 29-Callan; 30-Proctor, Callan; 31-Murello; 32-Allen.

Hunger for Bread
33-Taylor; 35-Murello; 36 All-Callan; 37 All-Callan; 38 All-Callan; 39-Taylor, Murello; 40-Taylor; 41-Murello; 42-Taylor; 43-Taylor; 44-Callan; 45 All-Taylor; 46-Allen; 47 All-Taylor; 48-Taylor; 49-Callan; 50-Taylor.

Hunger for Freedom and Justice
51-Callan; 53-Taylor; 54-Callan; 55-Taylor; 56-Taylor; 57 All-Taylor; 58 All-Taylor; 59 All-Taylor; 60-Mason, Callan; 61-Mason, Callan, Callan; 62-Taylor; 63-Mason; 64-Murello; 65-Murello; 66-Callan, Taylor; 67-Callan; 68-Taylor.

Hunger for the Spirit
69-Callan; 71-Murello; 72 All-Murello; 73-Murello, Callan; 74-Taylor; 75-Murello; 76-Callan; 77-Taylor; 78-Taylor; 79-Taylor; 80 All-Murello; 81-Mason, Murello; 82-Murello; 83 All-Murello; 84-Murello; 85-Murello; 86-Murello.

Hunger for the Truth
87-Callan; 89-Taylor; 90-Murello; 91-Murello; 92-Murello; 93-Taylor; 94-Murello; 95-Taylor; 96-Murello; 97 All-Taylor; 98-Taylor, Murello, Murello; 99 All-Taylor; 100-Murello, Callan; 101-Murello; 102-Callan, Murello; 103-Murello, Callan; 104-Taylor.

Hunger for Understanding
105-Callan; 107-Murello; 108 All-Taylor; 109-Taylor, Callan, Taylor; 110-Taylor; 111 All-Taylor; 112-Murello; 113 All-Taylor; 114-Taylor, Callan; 115-Callan, Taylor; 116-Murello; 117-Murello; 118-Taylor; 119-Taylor; 120 All-Murello; 121 All-Callan; 122-Taylor.

Hunger for Peace
123-Murello; 125-Murello; 126 All-Murello; 127-Taylor, Murello; 128-Taylor; 129-Murello; 130-Taylor; 131-Taylor; 132 All-Taylor; 133 All-Taylor; 134 All-Taylor; 135-Taylor, Murello; 136-Callan, Murello, Murello; 137-Murello, Taylor; 138-Murello; 139-Murello; 140-Callan.

Hunger for Jesus
141-Allen; 143-Taylor; 144-Taylor; 145-Callan; 146-Callan; 147-Mason, Taylor; 148-Taylor; 149 All-Taylor; 150-Allen; 151-Allen, Murello; 152-Callan; 153-Murello.